SLP TO BE

AN UNOFFICIAL GUIDE TO GETTING INTO GRADUATE SCHOOL FOR SPEECH-LANGUAGE PATHOLOGY

AUTHOR:
MICHAEL CAMPBELL, M.S. SLP

EDITOR:
MEG (RADIUS) BURIK

Michael Campbell

SLP To Be:
   An Unofficial Guide to Getting Into Graduate School for
      Speech-Language Pathology

First edition July 2020

Author: Michael Campbell
Editor: Meg (Radius) Burik (www.radiusb.com)
Cover Design: Sandamali Kamalchandra (hyperx_art on Instagram)
Layout Design: Adammyhr (www.adammyhr.com)

Belmar
Learning, LLC

www.belmarlearning.com

CONTENTS

CHAPTER 4
Getting Ready to Write Your Essay   33

CHAPTER 5
Writing The First Draft   41

CHAPTER 6
Revising and Improving   47

CHAPTER 7
Letters of Recommendation   61

PREFACE

The best way to use this book is to read it all the way through before completing the tasks in each chapter. There may be sections that do not seem to apply to you, but you should read them anyway as they contain important notes that relate to other chapters. This approach will give you an overview of the process and a sense of what you are working towards. Once you have read the book in its entirety, start over and complete the tasks in each chapter before moving on to the next.

Plan to write several drafts of your essays. If you are pressed for time because you procrastinated, relax. You can still write strong essays and get into graduate school. But you will need to be especially disciplined as you work.

The goal of this book is two-fold. First, it aims to demystify the process of applying to and earning acceptance into graduate school for speech-language pathology (abbreviated SLP), though many of these techniques could be applied to other fields. Second, it is a guide to producing high-quality applications. Note: it is a guide not a recipe.

Do not allow this guide to replace personalized advice from professors (especially those in the field of communication disorders), advisors, admissions counselors, or other knowledgeable experts. Allow this guide to better prepare you to work with them and to learn from their wisdom. The more you know about the process when you speak with them, the more they will be able to spend time with you on things that really make a difference to your chances.

CHAPTER 1

CHOOSING A SCHOOL OR PROGRAM

You have over three hundred options for graduate studies in speech-language pathology. Yes, that is a lot of schools to choose from. Sorting through so many options is overwhelming and time-consuming, but it is critical to finding a school that you can get into and that will help you thrive.

Before even looking at schools, you need to determine what is important to you. If you jump into ASHA's EdFind and start wading through websites, you'll soon get turned around and become overwhelmed.

This will require some introspection and analysis of your life goals. Light some candles, grab a glass of wine (or your preferred beverage), and give yourself a few hours to think about what you're truly expecting from graduate education.

WHAT IS IMPORTANT TO YOU?

Take some time to think about each of the following considerations and decide if it is important to you. Every person has different life circumstances and expectations of graduate school, so consider your unique situation. As you read through, create a separate list of the things that are most important to you.

Clinical Placements

RELATED to program emphasis are clinical placements. Some might even go so far as to say that your clinical placements are more valuable than any specialized classes. Regardless, this may be an important factor for you. For example, if you are certain that you'd like to work in a medical setting, you will want a school that offers those kind of clinical placements. This will give you valuable experience and help you establish relationships with professionals who can mentor you. Not all programs guarantee clinical placements in all settings. If you're not sure what area you are interested in, consider a school that will guarantee a placement in each of the major settings: school, medical, and private practice.

Traditional / Online / Hybrid

FOR any number of reasons that only you can know, you might be looking for an online program. Perhaps you're living abroad and looking to start your degree before moving to the U.S. Maybe you have children and need some extra flexibility in your schedule and a hybrid program is your best fit. Think carefully about what matters to you. The pros and cons of traditional vs online programs is beyond the scope of this book.

Full-Time / Part-Time

GENERALLY speaking, attending school full-time is your best option. You will finish in the shortest amount of time and be able to start earning your salary sooner. For many people, this is not possible and a part-time program is the perfect solution. Also consider if the program will allow changes to your plan. Do you have a medical condition that may slow you down? Do you have children and you need to be able to postpone a class? It is important to know how flexible a program is before you apply. This is something you will likely have to ask the program's graduate advisor.

Program Specialization

ALL accredited programs in SLP will provide you the same basic education with little variation. Programs must offer coursework and clinical experiences that meet the same national standards that every other program must meet. That said, many programs try to have some kind of unique offering. If you already know that you want to work with a specific disorder or population, find a school that specializes in it. Also, you might already have a preference for medicine or education. Schools sometimes offer elective classes or certifications to help prepare you for work in those specialized areas.

Leveling Options

IF you are an out-of-field student (meaning you have a bachelor's degree in a field that is not related to Speech & Hearing Sciences), you'll either need to complete a post-baccalaureate program, a second degree, or select a master's program that includes leveling course work in the graduate degree.

Geographic Area

Do you want to be near home? In a big city or in a small town? If you are able to move for graduate school, at least consider the option. The market for higher education, especially at the graduate level, is national. If you limit yourself to an area, state, or region, you're limiting your competitiveness.

An anecdote on being willing to move:

"I worked with two other girls as an SLPA [Speech-Language Pathology Assistant] who all wanted to go to graduate school. We all had our preferences for schools in a big city, near home, near a boyfriend, etc. At the end of the day, two of us were willing to compromise and go to any school that we got into. The girl who wasn't willing to move, is not a speech-language pathologist today."

~Treasyri, SLP

School Size

ARE you looking to be part of a huge community of tens of thousands of students or do you feel more at home on a smaller campus? Generally speaking, larger schools have more resources in all areas but smaller schools can provide a more personalized experience.

Program Size

THE size of the graduate program is more important than the size of the university. Do you want to be one of five students in a cohort? This will mean infinitely more contact with professors and you will be forced to work a lot with the same people. If you want more independence, consider a larger cohort of twenty-five to one hundred students. Program size affects many factors: amount of funding, the number of faculty you'll work with, average class size, etc.

Research Opportunities

IF you think a PhD is in your future, you'll definitely want some research experience during your master's program. Even if you aren't interested in pursuing a PhD, working on research is a great way to deepen and enrich your understanding of topics that are important to you. It can absolutely have an impact on your clinical career. This means you may want a program with opportunities for student research as well as faculty members that are interested in the same topics as you.

Degree Type

Do you want to be a clinician working with clients or are you looking for a non-clinical career path? Be sure that your school offers the specific degree you're looking for *and* that it is accredited. If you're looking to practice, make sure that your degree will qualify you to earn your Certificate of Clinical Competence (CCC or "C's" for short). If the program is not accredited, it is not going to help you become a practicing SLP.

State Certification

IF you know that you want to work in Minnesota, then a graduate program in Minnesota will be able to help you obtain the necessary state licenses. That said there is such a high demand for SLP's that most employers will help you through the certification process regardless of where your degree is from.

———————

So with that list of considerations in mind (along with any other factors you've determined are important), go and meditate! Think about what you want from your grad program. Decide what the "make it or break" it factors are.

Typically you only need one or two criteria to help narrow down your selection to a reasonable number of possible schools. Consider ranking the criteria from most to least important, that way you can adjust your search as you go.

On being flexible:

"Getting into grad school is like a relationship. If the guy has to be 6 foot 6, master's degree, six-figure salary, blue eyes... you might not have a man. Unlike on TV, you can't be the overweight bald man going with the super hot wife. Grad school is similar. You can't have a 3.1 GPA but want a big-name program on the beach in California with funding and a research spot. Sometimes you might have to find the no-name school in the little backwoods of somewhere that will see your potential and want to make an investment in you. And you do your time. I went to the school that let me in, and I got my little piece of paper. And today I'm doing what I love."

~Treasyri, SLP-CCC

Making Your List of Programs

Once you have decided what criteria are important to you, you need to begin compiling a list of possible programs. Literally, you're just going to be writing names of schools on a piece of paper or typing them into an excel document. Aim for a list of approximately 30 schools that might be good options for you.

While it is tempting to blindly pick programs based on rankings, it is probably not the best strategy. Here are some better options to find qualified programs:

1. **ASHA's EdFind search service:** http://www.asha. org/edfind/: The information available on this website is submitted by academic programs to the American Speech and Hearing Association. It is very detailed and is the best place to start your search.

2. **Professor Recommendation:** Professors in the field are constantly working with faculty at other schools, keeping in touch with former students, and following research coming out of different programs. Even professors from other related fields may be able to point you in the right direction as you search for a program that fits your interests and needs.

3. **Alumni & Current Students:** Your undergraduate institution can very likely put you in touch with alumni who are studying (or studied) SLP at the graduate level. Start by asking older classmates if they know where other people went to graduate school. If you're interested in a specific school, ask if your classmates or professors happen to know someone there. Students currently in programs can give you great information on what it is like actually there and working with the faculty.

4. **Practicing SLP's:** If you know any current speech-language pathologists, ask where they studied. Ask where their colleagues studied. Maybe they are still in touch with faculty at programs.

5. **Search engines:** A simple search online for keywords related to "graduate school" and "speech language pathology" is a great place to start. You might benefit by reading personal blogs of people who went to specific schools.

6. **Social Media:** There are many groups on Facebook and hashtags on Twitter related to becoming a Speech Language Pathologist. Other online platforms include TheGradCafe and Reddit, but there are always new places where students gather online. Find a platform and be willing to reach out and get involved in the conversations happening there. Finally, many graduate programs also have a social media presence where you can get a small sense of what goes on there; try following them.

THE HARD PART: NARROWING THE LIST

Just because you heard about a program somewhere doesn't mean it will 100% meet the criteria you set earlier, nor does it mean you'll be able to get in there. This is no time for love at first sight. This is where the real work begins.

What you've got to do now is look up each individual school and get the details. If your list is long, you'll have to "paint with a broad brush" during this first round of research. For the most part, you'll want to Google the name of the university and "SLP" or something similar. That should get you to the official program website.

Start by verifying that the school meets the major criteria you set earlier (i.e., specialization, location, etc).

Unfortunately, some schools do not maintain very up-to-date websites. As a technology lover, I find that to be incredibly irritating. If during your online research you decide that a school doesn't meet your major criteria, cross it off your list. If you need more information, don't be afraid to call the school. Email is also an option, but you tend to get slower responses without as much detailed information. I recommend trying to set up a call with a professor, graduate advisor, or the department chair if at all possible.

At this point, it is worth considering "the numbers" like GPA and GRE scores.

Minimum Requirement vs Average

The *minimum requirement* is just what you would expect: the lowest possible score the school will consider accepting. The *average* is calculated (usually) based on the previously admitted cohort but is *not* a requirement for acceptance.

Keep in mind, very few schools publish *required minimums.* However, many schools will make their *average data* available, at least on ASHA's EdFind. Either piece of data is very useful for your planning.

If your GPA/GRE score is lower than the minimum, your application *will automatically be rejected. Do not waste your time and money applying to schools where you do not meet the minimum standard.* The numbers are cut and dry ways to get rid of candidates who do not meet the requirements.

If you're GPA/GRE score is lower *than the average,* don't despair! Remember how averages work: almost *half* of the cohort (or more!) could have a GPA lower than the average.

Program Fit

APPLICANTS often underestimate the importance of *program fit* when creating their list of schools to apply to. Understanding program fit can help you dramatically increase your chances of getting into a program.

Here's how it works:

Each school/graduate program is made up of faculty members. These are often professors with a PhD (which is a highly specialized research degree) as well as instructors with master's degrees who may teach and also supervise students doing clinical work. Each of these people has specific interests within the field of SLP. Their interest might be as broad as "child language assessment" or as specific as "factors affecting speech intelligibility of people with hypokinetic dysarthria."

Imagine for a moment you are a faculty member who has spent the past fifteen years researching the use of *delayed auditory feedback* in people who stutter. Your colleague Dr. Jefferson has been researching how *alternative and augmentative communication can support individuals with autism spectrum disorder.* Another colleague, Dr. Smith, is conducting an experiment on *grammatical morpheme acquisition in bilingual Spanish/English children.*

Now imagine you, as a faculty member, are reviewing three applications for graduate school. You can only accept one of the following:

- **Applicant A** is desperately interested in stuttering and fluency disorders in bilingual Spanish/English speakers.

- **Applicant B** wants to become an SLP because they "want to help people."

- **Applicant C** is interested in language disorders resulting from traumatic brain injuries.

Assuming all three applicants have similar GPA's, GRE scores, and letters of recommendation, the choice is obviously Applicant A. They're the only person who has interests that align with faculty at the institution. Applicant B "wants to help people" which is true of nearly every speech-language pathologist and not something that will help you stand out. Applicant C has a really defined interest, but there is no faculty member with similar interests who can mentor them.

Faculty interest and expertise are some of the biggest factors that influence fit, but they're not everything. Geography, personality, local culture, focus on a certain setting, can all contribute to how well you fit into a program. For example, if you have an intense interest in rural health care, a program at an urban university is likely not the best fit. Read about the department and the university as a whole when trying to determine program fit.

Once you narrow your list down to ten to fifteen schools, it's time to do some more decision-making.

HOW MANY SCHOOLS SHOULD I APPLY TO?

B ased on your specific circumstances, consider the following:

1. **How many applications can you afford?** There are application fees, transcript fees, the cost of sending GRE scores, and other incidental costs. Don't spend more than you can afford on applications.

2. **How many schools do you *qualify* for?** Don't apply to any schools that don't match your qualifications. If you have a 3.0 GPA, applying only to top ranked programs is not a good idea. Be strategic. Consider applying to a few "reach" schools that you know would be difficult to get into as well as to several schools where you stand a better chance.

3. Applying to schools in a **broad geographic area** (multiple states and regions) might help boost your chances. Graduate education is a national market. What makes you unique will change based on where a program is located (more on this in chapter 4).

4. Applying to **four to eight schools is fairly typical**, though there are people who only apply to one. The most I've ever seen someone apply to is sixteen! Applying to more schools generally equates to more (not necessarily better) chances to be accepted.

CHAPTER 2

PLANNING & MANAGING YOUR APPLICATIONS

After you have decided which schools to apply to, you will need a system to manage your applications. Even just two or three applications have many pieces and moving parts to track. This chapter offers some tips as well as two examples of how you can manage the application process; one is computer-based and the other is paper-based. If neither of them works for you, come up with a system that will work for you.

Most importantly, once you get a system, stick to it. Don't waste more time than necessary coming up with the perfect system. Simple is best.

But before you even get to that, you'll want to put together a quick-reference cheat sheet.

QUICK-REFERENCE CHEAT SHEET

Many applications will ask you for the same information over and over again, for example, the dates of attendance at every college or university you have attended. You will waste *a significant* amount of time if you have to look things up every single time.

Create a quick-reference sheet with all the information you need for different parts of your application. Keep it close at hand as you fill out applications to make the process go more quickly.

You will need:

- **Education History:** If you have credit from multiple universities (including AP, dual-credit, summer classes, etc., include the following for each:

  - Dates of enrollment (e.g., Aug 2018-May 2019 or Fall 2018 – Spring 2019)
  - Number of credit hours completed
  - GPA
  - GPA: Last 60 credit hours

- **Transcripts:**

  - Have unofficial transcripts ready in PDF format and saved in a folder called "Unofficial Transcripts" in case a school will accept unofficial in place of official ones. Name each file with the school name and associated transcript (e.g. "Truman State Unofficial Transcript")
  - If *official* transcripts are required, you'll request those online through your university. Get a link to the request website or form. Bookmark it for quick reference.

- **Basic Contact Information**
- **Resume / Curriculum Vitae**
- **Contact information for recommenders**

  - Email,
  - Phone,
  - Title,
  - Relationship,
  - Years Known

- **GRE scores**
- **Logins / Usernames / Passwords**
    - You'll be creating many different online logins. Create a word document or spreadsheet to keep track of all the passwords and usernames you're creating.

A COMPUTER-BASED SYSTEM

This is one way you can consider organizing yourself as you are applying to graduate school. Make one master, dedicated folder on your computer called "Grad School Applications." Within it, store copies of everything you need as you're applying to graduate school. In this folder, make 5 subfolders:

1. GRE Prep

2. Personal Statement Drafts

3. Recommenders

4. Schools

5. Transcripts

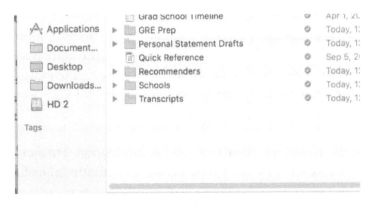

This is one example of how to organize your files

Each folder contains different information or tools related to the process.

1. **<u>GRE Prep</u>:** Store anything related to preparing for the GRE. Things you might keep include: a copy of your study schedule, receipts for books, copies of test scores, and a list of all the school codes you need to send your scores to.

2. **<u>Personal Statement Drafts</u>:** Store all of the drafts of your personal statement, including all of the prewriting activities (in subfolder). Just name them "Draft 1", "Draft 2", etc. to keep them in order. As covered in later chapters, you *must* customize your personal statement for each school, but this folder offers you a place to keep the "master template." More on that will be covered in later chapters.

3. **<u>Recommenders</u>:** Make a subfolder for each recommender. Also keep a copy of the cover letter, resume, and personal statement you send to them. Some of your recommenders may let you have a copy of the letters they submit on your behalf, so keep those here too.

4. **<u>Schools</u>:** Create a subfolder for each school you're applying to. In it, keep copies of receipts for application fees, confirmation emails, and a full copy of your application for reference.

5. **<u>Transcripts</u>:** Many schools will accept unofficial transcripts for the application process. This can save you a lot of money if you have credits from several schools. Keep PDF's of the unofficial transcripts here for easy access as you're applying to schools.

Finally, the most important tool is *The Application Tracker*. You can create your own version in a spreadsheet application (like Excel). Or if you visit www.thespeechblog.com/resources you can access a downloadable version of the one I used.

If you're applying to more than one or two schools, the application process will quickly become unmanageable without a system in place. You do *not* want an automatic rejection because you forgot to send a transcript or GRE score. If you reliably and faithfully update this spreadsheet, you will feel more at ease about the status of each of your applications.

Label the rows with each school you're applying to. Label the columns with important information to remember. Below is a list of column headers you might consider using. Remember, not all of these categories will apply to every school (for example, T.C. Columbia does not require a GRE score).

- University
- Location
- Notes (misc extras like, "neat study abroad program" or "Friend Susan went there").
- Identified faculty (include people you'd be interested in speaking with or whose research aligns with your interests)
- Average GPA
- Average GRE
- Date Application Opens
- Deadline to Submit
- Application Fee
- Unofficial Transcripts OK? (YES or NO)
- Personal Statement Word/Page Limit
- Link to Online Application Login
- Username
- Password
- Date Submitted
- Date Fee Paid
- Personal Statement Uploaded
- Transcript 1 Sent/Uploaded
- Transcript 2 Sent/Uploaded
- Transcript 3 Sent/Uploaded

- GRE Score sent/received

- Letter of Rec Status: (recommender's name)

- Letter of Rec Status: (recommender's name)

- Letter of Rec Status: (recommender's name)

With this spreadsheet, you can easily check lots of information quickly. The key to making this work is to update it constantly as information becomes available. If you get an email saying your GRE scores were received - update the spreadsheet. If your recommender calls to tell you they sent their letter - update the spreadsheet. You *must* update the spreadsheet constantly so that you can trust the information in it.

Another tip to make this system even more powerful: use color coding. A simple red, yellow, green system is effective. For example, in the "GRE sent/received" column you would start with the boxes colored red. When you send the scores, type "Sent on 10/15/18" and color the box yellow. As soon as the school confirmed they have received the GRE scores, changed the text to "Received" and color it green. This will make it easy to visually scan your spreadsheet and see quickly which components need to be taken care of, are in progress, or complete. When a school is "all green" you can relax and know your application there is complete!

A Paper-Based System

Most applications are digital. This means that if you want to keep paper files, you'll end up doing a lot of printing. But if paper is more comfortable for you, then feel free to create a paper-based system.

Get a binder for each school and one for "everything else." On the front of each, you'll want to create an easy checklist for the steps to completing an application to that school. You'll need to include a lot of information, but how you set it up is up to you. Inside of the binder, keep everything that is unique to that school (personal statements, receipts, confirmation emails, etc).

In the "everything else" folder, I recommend keeping a copy of your unofficial transcripts, the transcript request form for official transcripts, a copy of the resume you're using (unless you customize it to each school), any information on your recommenders, and your *quick-reference cheat sheet.*

Here are some of the most important things you'll need to see at a glance (and so they should be include in your cheat sheet). I would suggest printing these onto a word document in an arrangement that makes sense to you, and keeping it on the inside cover of each folder. If you're ever not sure about the status of something, you can grab the binder for a specific school and quickly open it and find out what needs to be done. Finally, there is some information that might not be able (like the average GPA of those admitted to the program), and it is okay to skip these items.

- University Name:
- Location:
- Notes:
- Identified faculty:
- Average GPA admitted:
- Average GRE admitted:
- Date Application Opens:
- Deadline:
- Application Fee:
- Unofficial Transcripts OK?: (Yes/No)
- Statement word/page limit:
- Link to online application login:
- Username:
- Password:
- Date Submitted:
- Date Fee Paid:
- Personal Statement Uploaded:

- Transcript 1 Sent/Uploaded:

- Transcript 2 Sent/Uploaded:

- Transcript 3 Sent/Uploaded:

- GRE Score sent/received:

- Letter of Rec Status: (recommender's name):

- Letter of Rec Status: (recommender's name):

- Letter of Rec Status: (recommender's name):

With a system like this in place, you can quickly review how your application to a certain school is going. You must constantly update the checklist so that you can trust the information in it. If you get an email saying your GRE scores were received - print it, and update the checklist. If your recommender calls to tell you they sent their letter - update the checklist.

If you're applying to more than one or two schools, the application process will pretty quickly become unmanageable without a system in place. You do *not* want an automatic rejection because you forgot to send a transcript or GRE score.

STEP BY STEP

Once you have put a system in place, stick with it. Every time something changes with an application, change it in your system. You have to know you can trust and rely on whatever system you have created to contain accurate information.

With a system for organization in place, plan daily goals. On your calendar (be it paper, on the wall, or on your phone), add small tasks like "Check if UCLA received GRE score" or "Finish Univ of New Mexico Statement." Each day you can check off a few tasks and keep moving your applications forward. It might be painful, but the application process requires discipline to complete.

During a conversation with a professor about applying to graduate school, she joked that the process can be so complicated and time consuming that it can unintentionally but naturally filter out people who don't have good organization and time management skills.

Do *not* let your application get automatically rejected because you failed to organize yourself.

Chapter 3

What Happens to Your Application

You're going to spend dozens of hours preparing all aspects of your application. Then one day you'll click a button that says "Submit" and *your* part of the process will be finished. Knowing how to do your part well depends on understanding what happens to your application once you turn it in.

This chapter is a brief overview of the different processes your application may go through in a general way once you submit it. Keep in mind that the specifics will vary widely between universities.

Why is this chapter important?

If you understand how your application will be evaluated, you'll be better able to prepare it and ultimately boost your chances of getting an offer of admission.

From Submit to Decision

Once your application is received, the school will create a file for you. This may be digital or paper-based. As your letters of recommendation, GRE scores, and transcripts arrive, they will go into this file.

Once the application deadline passes, the school will probably look for incomplete applications (missing a GRE score or transcript) and immediately set them aside as automatic rejections. It may seem harsh, but the standards are in place for a reason, so make sure all of your materials arrive on time as the school requests. Do not leave anything until the last minute. At best, strive to have your applications complete two weeks before the deadlines. A departmental secretary, administrator, or a graduate assistant will likely do this sorting.

Once the school has all of the complete applications together, they'll begin reviewing. This process is different at every school. Some schools may review on a rolling basis (i.e. complete applications are reviewed as they arrive) or schools may wait for the application deadline to pass and review all applications at once.

Some schools receive very large numbers of applications and they may use some sort of "gatekeeper" or "cutoff" to narrow down the consideration pool. GRE scores and GPA are often used in this way. For example, a school might receive 400 applications. In the spirit of efficiency, the faculty could agree to reject the 100 applications with the lowest GRE scores or GPAs. Some universities, especially those that receive fewer applications, will give each application a holistic review.

Depending on the number of applications, a certain number of applications may be assigned to each faculty member. Some schools may ask all faculty members to read all applications. Some programs may have a committee of select faculty who read the entire pool. It depends on each school and the number of applications they receive. It is possible that only a few people will read your application.

Many schools have some sort of standardized evaluation template (that they will not publish) to review applications. It may ask readers to score each component on a scale of 1-5 or assign points for various parts of the application. This is the longest and most challenging part of the consideration process for schools. Once it is complete, the applications will likely be ranked from "strongest" to "weakest" using a coded system.

With the applications ranked, a school may begin to send out admission offers. Or they may interview a number of applicants for additional information. Interviews are also evaluated using a standardized metric, like the rest of the application. Again, these results will likely be ranked.

Once a school has a final list of ranked applications, it will consider the number of seats available in its program before sending admission letters. Say XYZ University has 20 spots in their graduate program. Some applicants will turn down the admission offers. So a school may take the list of 100 ranked applications, send admission letters to the first 30, and consider the next 20 or 30 to be the waiting list. As students accept or decline offers, schools then invite select applicants off of the waitlist.

An important note: If you are on a waitlist at a school, you could be offered admission up until the first day of classes. It seems crazy, but at the last minute a student may dropout of a program and open up a spot for someone else. If you're placed on a waitlist, it means your application was good enough, but there isn't room in the program to accept all qualified applicants. You should find this encouraging!

HOW THE DECISION IS MADE

The great secret of admissions: How to determine who gets in. The only people who know how the decision-making process works are the ones who are making the decision! And it varies greatly from institution to institution. Because of this variability and secrecy, there is a lot of speculation, rumor, and even myth.

In a very unofficial and unscientific way, we can split the decision into three parts:

1. The objective evaluation

2. The subjective evaluation

3. Chance

1. The Objective Evaluation

THE exact evaluation system used varies widely from university to university. Once you know which schools you are applying to, review their websites for evaluation information.

Here's an example of "objective" processes:

1. Applications are distributed to a pool of readers (evaluators).

2. Using a weighted point system that favors certain components of the application over others, each reader assigns a score to an application.

3. The scores from all readers of an application are averaged.

4. The averaged scores are used to rank applications.

Improve your chances in objective evaluations by improving your GPA and your GRE scores. Numbers like these are less subjective than other components of the application.

2. The Subjective Evaluation

A significant portion of the evaluation process is subjective, because humans. These are not "official" or even "intentional" criteria, but they do affect your application. What goes into this part?

- The reader's personal feelings, thoughts, and opinions
- The current political and economic climates
- Race and ethnicity of applicant
- The administrator in charge of putting your application together
- How your personality is perceived in your applications as well as any emails and phone calls

How do you improve your chances in subjective evaluations? That is a hard question to answer. Start by keeping in mind that anytime you're interacting with someone from the program you are being evaluated, judged, measured, and weighed. Officially? No. Unofficially? Yes. Sometimes it isn't even conscious or intentional!

Let's imagine two opposite scenarios:

- **Scenario 1:** You meet the departmental secretary when you're touring the department. There's a problem: the professor you're meeting with is running very late. You get snarky with the secretary. If she recognizes your name when she receives your application, do you think she'll have any patience as she checks to make sure your application is in order? What if she casually comments to one of the admissions committee members as she hands off the file, "Yea, I remember this name. They kept complaining about having to wait for Dr. Monroe." It's not a make or break issue, but it could negatively affect the evaluation.

- **Scenario 2:** While you're waiting for your tour you have a nice chat with the department secretary. You find out you both ran the same marathon. If she remembers your name when your application rolls in, maybe she'll smile when she sees it and take an extra second to make sure everything is the right order before she hands it off for evaluation. During lunch with a faculty member, the secretary mentions your shared love of marathons and how it was nice to meet you. Now, I'm not saying this professor will magically shout, "They're IN!" but having that professor think of you positively when they get your application puts you at an advantage.

These scenarios are imagined but they demonstrate the importance of characteristics like professionalism, kindness, civility, and respect throughout the application process (and life).

3. Chance

THIS is the worst part because you cannot really do anything about it. Maybe the day your GRE score arrives the secretary is out of the office and student worker accidentally misfiles it, making your application look incomplete. Maybe the year you apply to the school, there happen to be a bunch of braniac-super-students applying and while your 3.5 GPA is very strong, it does not look as good *relatively* speaking. Maybe the professor who is reading your application just had a meeting with a rude student and is now feeling frustrated and irritable, and so they're not as lenient when they see a typo in your essay.

Most of these things are impossible to account for but it is important to know that they're part of the application process. Now you understand the importance of planning ahead and getting things in early to help avoid minor issues. Remember, if your application is rejected, chance is part of the process and it is worth trying again.

TWO DECISION MAKING CASE STUDIES

Case Study 1: New Mexico State University

NEW Mexico State University is a large, public university in *Las Cruces, New Mexico*. The school is ranked #106th for its SLP program by US News & World Report (in case that matters to you).

They published a 1.5 page PDF document in 2014 explaining (briefly) how they will evaluate applications to their SLP program.

Here is a table that basically summarizes how all of their reviewers are instructed to score applications:

Grade Point Average (factor of 2)		Average GRE Scores (Verbal + Quant)		GRE Analytical Writing		Letters of Recommendation	Personal Statement	Resume
RATING	GPA	RATING	PERCENTILE	RATING	SCORE	RATING	RATING	RATING
5	3.75-4.00	5	55th +	5	5-6	5	5	5
4	3.50-3.74	4	50-54th	4	4	4	4	4
3	3.25-3.49	3	45-49th	3	3	3	3	3
2	3.16-3.24	2	40-44th	2	2	2	2	2
1	3.00-3.15	1	35-39th	1	1	1	1	1

These are the criteria NSMU used according to its website as of 2014; standards may have changed since publication.

Other key insights we can glean from the report include:

- *"The undergraduate GPA may be computed on the last 40 hours of coursework in a communication disorders major if appropriate. For students without an undergraduate CD major, only a cumulative GPA will be used."* This is probably good for most CD majors!

- *"At least two of the three letters of reference must be from professors in your major."* This emphasizes how important academic LOR's are.

- *"The GPA rating will be multiplied by a factor of 2"* This is good or bad depending on your GPA.

The most opaque and intriguing part of the document is this:

- "The CD Program Graduate Admissions Committee may consider multiple factors in addition to the application for admission score in order to determine who will be admitted to the program."

What does that mean?
I can think of three possible meanings:

1. The admissions committee reserves the right to override the other criteria if they think it's necessary based on something particularly outstanding. For example a history of plagiarism, an especially impressive personal statement, a top GRE score with a low GPA, etc.

2. They may consider "other stuff" like interviews, campus visits, and "unmentionables" like race, gender, socioeconomic status, gut feelings, social media profiles, etc.

3. The department is "covering its butt" in case they make a decision that appears incongruent with their published policy.

Case Study 2: San Francisco State University

San Francisco State University (SFSU) is a public university in San Francisco, California. SFSU is ranked #84 in SLP according to US News & World Reports.

The department publishes this statement in their Frequently Asked Questions section of their website regarding the five criteria they use to evaluate an application:

> Each faculty member individually reviews each applicant's file and rates the applicant using a 1-5 scale. Ratings of all faculty members are combined and the applicants are rank ordered. Applicants are rated across five areas of equal weight:
>
> 1. Academic Performance: Examples of sources of information for academic performance include academic transcripts and letters of recommendation from an academic source.
>
> 2. Writing Skills: Examples of sources of information for writing skills are the applicant's performance on the writing requirement and quality of writing in the applicant's application materials.
>
> 3. Clinical Potential: Clinical potential refers to the demonstration of professional qualities that are important for the practice of speech-language pathology, such as strong communication skills, good interpersonal skills, respect for individuals with diverse abilities. 'The Essential Functions Guide' describes the essential characteristics necessary for success in the SLP field.
>
> 4. Commitment to Diversity: Applicants must demonstrate a commitment to the promotion of diversity and respect for individuals of different

ages, gender, race, religions, sexual orientation, language backgrounds, cultural backgrounds, and socioeconomic backgrounds.

5. Recommendations: Letters from individuals who can speak to the applicant's potential for success with graduate studies in the CD field. At least one letter should be from an academic source.

These are the criteria SFSU used according to its website as of 2020; standards may have changed since publication.

Without more specific information on what they look for within each criteria, we cannot really make a complete evaluation chart for this one. BUT, you can review your own applicant profile to ensure that you cover or at least allude to these areas.

Under "Clinical Potential," there is a reference to *The Essential Functions Guide* which was published in 2007 by the *Council of Academic Programs in Communication Sciences and Disorders.* The abbreviated version that SFSU refers to lists 34 different functions one must be able to perform to be an SLP. The SFSU version is available at thespeechblog.com/resources

Here are a few highlights from that list:

- Display mature empathetic and effective professional relationships by exhibiting compassion, integrity, and concern for others.

- Self evaluate, identify, and communicate limits of one's own knowledge and skill to appropriate professional level and be able to identify and utilize resources in order to increase knowledge.

- Modify communication style to meet the communication needs of clients, caregivers, and other persons served.

Chapter 4

Getting Ready to Write Your Essay

One of the most critical components of your application is your *personal statement.* Trying to explain in a few hundred words why you want to become a Speech Language Pathologist is not an easy thing. Also a personal statement is not like other academic essays you have written; it has a different structure and flow.

This chapter contains exercises and pre-writing activities you should complete before writing your personal statement.

The point of these activities is to *get your creative juices flowing* and create a pool of ideas. This brainstorming phase will make writing your essay easier, give you ideas to customize it for each school, and even help prepare you for interviews! Answer every question – even if you *know* that answer will *never* go into your final personal essay. As you're writing don't worry about grammar, flow, or trying to sound smart.

Finding a Way to Stand Out

Anyone who has ever been on an admissions committee will tell you that eventually all of the essays run together. Imagine a professor needs to read a few dozen essays to find the best candidates. After an hour or so of essay reading, her eyes glaze over and she never wants to read the word "passion" or the phrase "language is what makes us human," again. This is not even a hypothetical situation— the two previous examples of clichés were taken from a conversation with a professor on this very topic.

A great essay will catch the readers' interest from the first sentence and motivate them to keep reading. Many strong writers use something unique to hook their readers - something to pique interest and break the monotony. Note: it is important that this opening does not sound glib or superficial.

Prewriting Activity:

List 10 things that make you unique. Write a paragraph about each of those things. If you get stuck, consider the following questions:

- What is the most unique thing about you?
- What makes you unusual?
- Do you have an interesting family history?
- Have you taken any unique trips?
- Were you raised in a way that makes you different?
- Do you speak multiple languages?
- Do you have a special talent or skill?

Think about what will make you interesting *to the reader* and in comparison to the other applicants. The small town with one stop light that I grew up in would really stand out in applications to schools in big cities. Do you know how to make balloon animals? That's unique. Write it down. Will it go into your essay? Most likely not, but this is a pre-writing activity.

Also, it is *okay* to include highly personal information here in this brainstorming that would *never* make it into your final essays.

Finally, I know that it can be difficult to see what is unique about yourself because you spend all day with yourself! You probably think of every aspect of your life as routine. It isn't! If you're really stuck, try asking a friend for help. Or imagine you're at a party where you know no one – what will you say about yourself to break the ice?

YOUR INTELLECTUAL INFLUENCES

Graduate school is an academic and intellectual pursuit. The field of SLP has a heavy focus on helping and serving others, yet it is still *graduate school* where you will be pursuing an advanced degree. The things that have influenced you intellectually are relevant and deserve some reflection.

Prewriting Activity:

REFLECT on the following questions. Write a paragraph response to each.

- What does speech-language pathology mean to you?
- Who were/are your favorite professors? Why?
- What was the best essay or project in school that you worked on? Why?
- What is the single most important concept you learned in school in general? What about in your degree area? In your favorite SLP-related class?
- What are some of the central ethical questions in the field of SLP? What is your position on them?
- What areas of specialty are you interested in within SLP? Why?
- Did you have any specific experiences that made you interested in SLP?
- Did you (or do you still) have any reservations or fears about entering the field? What are they? What might be underlying those fears?
- Have you completed any observation hours? What did you learn from them?

The Professors & People Who Have Influenced You

Academia in many ways is like a family tree. My undergraduate thesis advisor told me about his PhD advisor. As he explained to me the small circle of experts who trained him, it sounded like he was tracing back a sort of academic lineage. He learned from so-and-so who learned from so-and-so, etc.

Working with certain professors (whether taking their classes, reading their work, or working with them on a project) influences you and forms you as a scholar and future clinician. You pick up their perspectives and ways of viewing the field.

Prewriting Activity:

Reflect on the people who have influenced you and how you view the field of SLP (or related fields such as health care, linguistics, or education). Write a response to each question.

- Which professors have most influenced the way you think? What ideas or perspectives did they imprint upon you?

- Have any professors ever said something that stuck with you? What was it? Why did it stick?

- If you have completed any research, what was it about? What was your methodology? What did you learn from the process?

- Are there any professors who you would like to study under at a specific university?

- Is there a book or essay that you found particularly meaningful? Why?

WHEN DID YOU DECIDE ON SLP?

The moment you realized you wanted to become an SLP is a great source for personal statement inspiration. Some SLP's received language services as children and have never forgotten the impact their SLP made on their lives. Perhaps your own child has a language impairment and your interest grew out of that. Were you working in the corporate world until one day you arrived home, burnt out, and knew you wanted to start helping people? Maybe you're like me and you didn't have one singular moment that made you realize you wanted to get into this field – my decision to become an SLP was truly a journey.

Prewriting Activity:

WRITE at least half a page on the "moment" when you knew you wanted to be an SLP. When did you realize you wanted to become an SLP? Why?

Prewriting Activity:

WRITE about why you think you'd be a good SLP. Do you have any unique skills? What about previous personal or professional experiences?

LIFE AFTER GRAD SCHOOL

For the majority of graduate students in speech pathology, clinical work, rather than academia, is the end goal of a master's degree. Maybe you can use that as a source of inspiration for your personal statement.

Make a simple t-chart. On the left, list all of the reasons you want to become an SLP. Be *honest* – this is for you. On the right hand side of the t-chart list *other ways* you can satisfy that reason.

For example, if on the left you wrote, "Help young people

through education." Well, could you become an elementary school teacher? Maybe on the left you wrote, "I like language." On the right, you could write: Become a linguist; travel; become an ESL teacher. If you wrote, "earn a stable salary," on the left, what about "become a computer program" on the right?

The important thing here is to hold each reason in your mind, challenge it, and defend it! It is okay to create multiple drafts of theses lists as you work through this process. This will refine your motivation and help clarify things for you. When you step away at the end, you should have a much more clear idea of why speech-language pathology specifically is your chosen field.

CAN YOU HANDLE IT?

One of the most difficult and important questions the admissions committee must answer about each candidate is "Can she/he be successful in graduate studies?" You should take some time to answer this question for yourself. To make this activity worthwhile, you have to *brutally honest* with yourself. Find your weaknesses and pressure yourself to dig into them even if it is painful.

Many people often write in their personal statement things about their dedication to becoming an SLP, their passion for learning, their desire to help others, etc. To support those claims, you need evidence. The admissions committee is not going to go looking for that evidence; it is your job to show it to them.

Here are some questions to reflect on:

- Does your undergraduate background *truly & honestly* prove that you're ready for more intensive studies? Does your GPA? Which projects, classes, papers? What kind of study skills do you have?

- Do you have the relevant academic background to be successful at the graduate level? Can you remember the relevant principles from important pre-requisite classes?

- What have you done to prepare yourself for graduate school? (e.g., Classes, trainings, interviews, shadowing)

- What personal attributes do you have that will help you succeed in a masters program?

- Have you done anything equally as intense or challenging as graduate school? (Fellowships, training programs, degree in other areas, etc.)

- What evidence is there in your background that you want to become an SLP *and* that you can make it through graduate school?

BIGGEST ACCOMPLISHMENT TO DATE

Completing a master's degree is no easy thing. It is a significant achievement. Take some time to reflect on other things you have achieved in your life.

Prewriting Activity:

THINK about different aspects of your life: personal, professional, or academic. What achievement in your life are you most proud of? What did it take to achieve it? What did you learn? Would you do it again? How would you do it differently? Finally, of all the things you gained from that experience, which are relevant to graduate education?

Extra Credit: Answer the above question multiple times with different aspects of your life.

RESEARCH EXPERIENCE

The importance of hands-on research experience varies greatly from one program to another, but in general it is not a requirement for entry into most graduate programs for SLP. That said, if you have research experience it could be very helpful to you in the application process.

Prewriting Activity:

START by making a list of research projects in which you have been involved in any capacity. Be sure to note your role and participation. It is okay if your role was relatively minor; don't exaggerate. Professors are expert researchers and they will quickly see through overstated claims.

Next, think about and then write about what you learned from the research. Feel free to mention practical things and also overarching concepts. This type of self-reflection is very important. It is something that you won't be given class time to do, but is expected you will do on your own.

Finally, try to articulate how that research affects the field. SLP has a strong focus on evidence-based best practices. It is important to be able to not only perform research but also understand how it informs clinical practice. If your research experience is in another area, that's okay! Think about how it may have affected practice in that field.

CHAPTER 5

WRITING THE FIRST DRAFT

This chapter is designed to get your first draft out of your head and onto the page. Be sure to complete the exercises in the previous chapter before your first draft.

This first draft should be totally from your heart. Don't think *what do they want to read?* Don't try to second-guess the committee. Write how you would speak. Don't overthink it. And don't stop to edit.

Here are three simple steps to get you through that first draft.

STEP 0: START EARLY

This should be pretty obvious, but I wrote it because… well… you need to start early! DO NOT wait until the last minute to write your essays. I repeat: DO NOT wait until the last minute to write your essays.

Best practice is to start writing your essays *about 6 months before they're due*. A successful candidate will start essays in June even if they're not due until January. This gives you plenty of time to revise your essays. And you will need to!

Step 1: Make sure you've done the prewriting exercises

If you think you can write your grad school admissions essay without doing a little planning, you're either 1) a hyper-focused prodigy, or 2) you need to rethink your decision to go to grad school. That might seem a little harsh, but let's not sugarcoat this:

Graduate school is a *huge* decision in every way possible (economically, socially, emotionally, professionally). You should spend time doing some "soul searching" to figure out why you want to go. Your conscious rationalization might not even match what is going on in your subconscious once you start really thinking about it. Further, graduate school will stretch and push your planning skills beyond most other previous experiences; you might as well start practicing.

In the first draft of an essay that I eventually used to win a prestigious international grant, I started with a (hackneyed) explanation of my passion for teaching, inspired by my wonderful high school Spanish teacher. After several months of revising with guidance from an amazing writing mentor, I was able to draw a *meaningful* thread through most major events in my life (literally from birth) and show how those antecedents, more than inspired me, compelled me to go abroad with this grant.

Ok, that's a little dramatic sounding – but it was truly an emotional and stirring experience. I even cried once… no joke! The pre-writing exercises in the previous chapter will get you to start thinking introspectively.

Nothing should be overlooked during this process. Look at everything you've done: jobs you've had, people who have mentored you, classes you've taken, books that have inspired you.

The point is, you really need to look inside yourself and reflect on what you find. So if you have not done it, go back a chapter and do the pre-writing activities.

Step 2: Set aside time

Set aside time for writing; not time to write while you're watching TV in the background or also babysitting, sweeping, working, gardening, or doing laundry. You need time for writing only.

Give yourself 30 minutes or an hour if you can. Create a quiet, relaxing space.

When I have to write and am unable to start, I set a timer and tell myself to write for at least 2 to 5 minutes. Writing for an hour seems impossible, but writing for few minutes is easy. This often breaks the ice and I end up writing for the whole hour. Try it!

Step 3: Word Vomit Everything

So you've done the pre-writing activities, you're starting early, and you've set aside some significant time to write. What do you do now? Word vomit.

You know that feeling when you open your mouth and words just start flowing uncontrollably? Maybe you're angry or nervous or excited, and you just can't seem to stop yourself until you've said everything in your head?

That's what you want to do for this first draft. You're just going to put pen to paper (or fingers to keyboard) and start writing the answer to the question: "Why do you want to pursue graduate studies in Speech Language Pathology?" without thinking or stopping or editing.

That's it. Just *start writing* the answer to the question "Why do you want to go grad school for SLP?"

You might think, "But that's not the prompt!" And you're right; it is probably not the exact prompt for every school. But I bet it is pretty close, and "pretty close" is good enough for this first draft.

Imagine you're sitting on a comfy couch having a cup of coffee (or wine or other delicious beverage) with someone who asks you why you're interested in the field. You've got nothing but time and someone who is super interested in your answer. Tell them everything!

Some rules for this step:

- Do not stop to edit at this point (Seriously! Don't waste your time. You'll be doing plenty of revising later.)
- Do not worry about length.
- Do not worry about using big words or sounding smart.

If you're having trouble writing, try recording yourself saying the answers out loud. Once you've said it all, listen to it and type it out (adding detail as necessary).

My super-rough-draft was three pages long and riddled with errors, errant thoughts, and all sorts of stuff that (while true) I would never show to grad schools. But the point was to get the answer onto paper! It didn't have any flow. Ideas jumped around. My first word-vomit-draft has weird sentences like:

- Becoming an SLP means I'll be able to get a decent paying job almost anywhere. If teacher's made better salaries, I wouldn't ever consider leaving teaching.
- I used to be terrified of becoming an SLP because I didn't know anything about working with people with disabilities.

During the word vomit phase, nothing is too small to exclude. During a conversation with my mentor about my essays for a study abroad grant, I mentioned that I was the only person in my family to have traveled to a foreign country. Her jaw dropped a little as she asked, "and why isn't that in your essay?" I went on to turn that seemingly useless fact into one of the cornerstones of my essay.

This is a perfect time to bring up any tough experiences you had growing up or in school. Mention anyone who has inspired you. Are you interested in SLP because it offers economic stability and job security? You can mention that in this draft!

Get specific! Talk about classes or professors that you loved (and why!) and classes you hated (and why!).

It is best to get this first word-vomitted-draft out all at once. Your ideas will be more connected and more complete. Once you get in the flow, don't stop! Just keep writing.

How will you know when you're finished? When you have

nothing left to say about why you want to become a speech and language pathologist. *Every* possible reason should be in that first draft, including ones you would *never* say or show to an admissions committee.

CHAPTER 6

REVISING AND IMPROVING

So you have your first draft straight from the heart. Awesome! Save it. Make a backup of it. Email it to yourself if you need to! And set it aside.

Let's start over with the writing thing.

Before you even start writing, an important vocabulary note: there are many names for a *statement of purpose*. Some schools make call it a *personal statement, personal essay, admissions essay, letter of intent,* or any number of other things. They are all basically the same thing.

Each school will specify a different essay prompt. But ultimately, a good admissions essay should answer the same essential questions. Other details should be included, but the bare essentials are:

1. How does your background qualify you for graduate studies?

2. Why do you want to attend our specific school to specifically study your chosen topic?

3. What do you plan to do after you graduate?

These questions are often not explicit, but readers expect to find the answers in your essay. The actual prompts might read something like:

- *Explain your interest in the field of Speech-Language Pathology.*

- *"Tell us about your intellectual curiosity in this field, describe how you plan to apply that curiosity to clinical practice, and tell us what makes you uniquely qualified to execute this plan." (University of Redlands, 2016)*

- *"Discuss the factors that led you to pursue studies in speech, language, and hearing sciences. You may comment on aspects of the discipline that interest you, insights gained from coursework, and clinical, research, or other personal experiences. - Describe your career goals." (University of Arizona, 2018)*

- *"There are no official guidelines for the letter, but we normally expect that it will include an explanation of why you wish to attend this graduate program and why you think you will succeed here. You can use the letter to highlight your strengths and experiences, explain discrepancies and tell us your goals." (University of New Mexico, 2015)*

Although most universities expect similar components to your essay, each one will ask in a slightly different way. I recommend reading all the prompts for the schools you're interested in. Once you've identified your top-choice, start with their essay prompt.

"I heard you shouldn't 'adapt' an essay, but that you should write a completely unique essay for each and every school"

You've probably also heard you should eat lots of vegetables and exercise at least 20- minutes everyday. But that doesn't mean you are doing it!

If you have the time and energy to write 6-10 totally different essays, then do it. Yes, they'll probably be slightly better. I say "slightly" better because remember how each school is expecting those same components in the personal statement? That means your answers will all basically be the same. With some good, vigorous editing we can customize each essay in a way that still matches each school's prompt and doesn't overwhelm you with multiple original essays.

The only other time I would recommend a unique essay is for a truly unique question. For example, sometimes schools use funny questions like "What three objects would you want with you while stranded on a deserted island?" or "If you were a kitchen utensil, what would you be and why?" to get a sense of how you react to and handle unique circumstances. Those prompts definitely call for unique answers.

Now that you have this one essay prompt/question that you're focused on for now, sit down and answer the question. If you're having trouble, use those essential questions above to create a simple outline that aligns with the prompt. Also, remember all that pre-writing from Chapter 4? Feel free to draw from it. This is the time to start mining for golden nuggets in the writing you've already done.

THE HOOK

Admission committees complain that many essays are too similar. One professor of Speech & Hearing Sciences confided, "If I have to read: *language is what makes us human* in a letter of intent one more time, I'm gonna barf!"

Finding a way to make your essay stand out boosts your chance of success. One great way to stand out is to write an engaging and original first line. Strong writers use something unique to hook their readers and break the monotony of reading essay after essay that starts: "My passion for Speech-Language Pathology comes from..." It is important that your opening is not glib or superficial— it should be something meaningful that gives your application a different tone or original feel.

Here are some of my favorite first lines from famous books to help get you warmed up!

- *"My suffering left me sad and gloomy." -The Life of Pi*

- *"You better not tell nobody but God." - The Color Purple*

- *It was the best of times, it was the worst of times, it was the age of wisdom, it was the age of foolishness, it was the epoch of belief, it was the epoch of incredulity, it was the season of Light, it was the season of Darkness, it was the spring of hope, it was the winter of despair." -A Tale of Two Cities*

- *"All happy families are alike; each unhappy family is unhappy in its own way." -Anna Karenina*

- *"Mr. and Mrs. Dursley, of Number Four Privet Drive, were proud to say that they were perfectly normal, thank you very much." -Harry Potter and the Sorcerer's Stone*

Now you're probably wondering how to write your *own* strong first line, right?

ACTIVITY:

MAKE a list of things that make you unique. Note: if you did the pre-writing activities, you should already have ideas to draw from.

If you get stuck, try answering the following questions:

- What is the most unique thing about you?

- What make you unusual?

- Do you have an interesting family history?

- Have you taken any trips?

- Were you raised in a way that makes you different?

- Do you speak multiple languages?

- What is "the cool thing" about yourself you like to tell new people?

- When people learn_____about you, they're usually surprised.

Keep in mind: you *do not* have to be the *first person ever* to have done something for it to be unique or interesting. Think about what would make you interesting to the reader compared to other people applying. For example, I grew up in a small town with one stoplight. Universities in rural Missouri won't find that interesting, but readers for schools in New York or Los Angeles could be intrigued by that anecdote. It isn't hugely relevant to graduate school, but it can make the essay stand out enough to get the reader to keep awake and interested.

One of my classmates in graduate school used her background as a salsa musician who traveled Latin America as part of her application essay. Another classmate used her experiences as a classroom teacher to set off her essay with a heart-warming tone.

Another thing to remember: it is *okay* to include highly personal information here in this brainstorming that would *never* make it into your final essays. The point is to get your creative juices flowing.

Finally, I know that it can be difficult to see what is unique about yourself because you spend all day with yourself! You probably think of every aspect of your life as routine. It isn't! If you're really stuck, ask a friend for help brainstorming.

CUT IT DOWN AND SHAPE IT UP

Congratulations! If you're at this point, you already have a lengthy first draft of your statement. The hardest part is over. Now you just need to refine, polish, and shape.

Your first draft is probably very, very long. That's great! But you need to cut it down. Ideally, you'll get it down to one-page or less.

How?

If you follow this process, you will end up with many drafts of your personal statement saved on your computer. I recommend having a separate folder. In that folder, name your first draft: "Draft 1." Make a copy of it and rename it "Draft 2." When you start revising, make changes to Draft 2 and leave Draft 1 alone. Eventually, you'll get to a point where you'll want to save Draft 2 as Draft 3 and so on and so forth. Why? Because you can revisit earlier drafts of your essay that might have information you cut out or replaced in a later draft. It makes it easier to fix things if you change your mind.

Now in a separate document, create an outline of your essay. Why? Because it needs to be organized to make sense.

Here are three very basic but highly functional sample outlines. Each section represents approximately a paragraph, but could be more or less depending on how it fits into your experiences. Also, don't be afraid to remove, add, or rearrange sections— this is your essay and should reflect your writing choices.

1. Outline by Function:

- Hook / Intro
- Professional Preparation
- Personal Preparation
- Academic Preparation
- Research Preparation
- How XYZ University will tie it all together

2. The Time Machine Outline

- Past
- Present
- Future

3. Outline of Your Journey

- The Epiphany Moment (or not)
- First Step
- Next Step
- Next Step
- The Future

As you look at these outlines you might think: "I already wrote stuff that fits into each of these sections!" So, guess what the next step is?

Take the material you've written previously and arrange it according to the outline you've chosen. You might have thoughts/anecdotes that don't fit in any section. That's fine. Ask yourself, "Does it really need to be in my essay?" If it really needs to be in the essay, decide if you need to adjust your outline to make space for it or adjust what you've written. You might need to add new content as well. That's fine too!

Following an outline will give your essay structure and shape. It ensures you don't forget key points.

Once your essay has some structure, start cutting it down. Each university sets its own standards for personal statements. Follow them. Generally, personal essays are between 500-1500 words, which is about 1-2 pages double-spaced. If your statement is already within that range, you probably don't need to cut it down. If not, take the time to get your essay under 1,000 words (or whatever the requirement is for the school you're applying to. It is always easy to add more to an essay, but it can be very difficult to cut it down. Start by looking for big sections that can be removed. Ask yourself...

- Is this idea necessary?
- What is the point of X paragraph? Can I combine the ideas into other paragraphs?
- Can I communicate this thought with fewer words?
- Am I trying to sound too smart? It might be using up too many words...
- Am I trying to brag or is this relevant?

As you're writing, you may reach a natural "stopping point" in which you want to save another copy of your draft. This way if you delete something, it is not lost forever. You can easily go back to it and add it back into your essay.

Writing at this point should be a cyclical process. As you finish going through each line of your essay, you'll start back at the beginning and do it again and again. Each time you'll gradually whittle down the essay.

When you get to the point where you've fully answered the prompt and are within the page limits, you're ready for the next key step.

FIND A MENTOR

You ~~cannot~~ should not try to do this on your own. Find a mentor to guide you.

Why? Because we get tunnel vision when reading our own writing. After a few passes we tend to skip things and to think it is a lot better than it actually is. Also, we're so close to our own lives that we sometimes can't make sense of it – a third party can make connections we take for granted.

The ideal mentor is...

- *A talented writer:* This is a tough and delicate thing to figure out. If the person is a professor, do they teach writing courses (good sign!)? Are they published? (good sign!) Do they often get asked to write letters of recommendation? (good sign!) Have they won grants in the past? (good sign!)?

- *Someone who works in the field:* Business people write differently than engineering people write differently than speech language pathologists. You want someone who knows your field and what is abuzz in its sphere of influence.

- *Someone who has experience with admissions essays:* Many of your college professors (even if they are from other fields) have probably served on an admissions review panel for graduate students before. These are the *perfect* people to give you advice on your essays because they know all of your competition and what reviewers will look for!

Those things describe the ideal writing mentor. The most important thing is to find someone you trust and who is willing to help you improve your writing. They need to offer open and honest feedback. It will do you no good if someone reads your essay and only says, "Yes, good work!" or "Everything sounds so good..."

Here are some people to consider ask for writing advice:

- An SLP you know

- Professors (from any field!)

- Your old high school teacher(s) / principals

- Career counselors (does your university have a career center?)

- Bloggers (especially those who blog about SLP)

- Friends (be careful though, you want *critical feedback* not just encouragement)

- Co-workers

As a final note, you don't have to know your mentor very well before beginning work with them. When I was applying for a Fulbright fellowship, I wrote to my academic advisor asking if he had any advice. He suggested I contact a different professor who "had some experience" with Fulbright. I wrote her a polite email asking if she could spare just a few minutes to chat with me about writing the essay. As it turns out, she is an alumnus of the program *and* a former member of the national selection committee! Her advice was AMAZING. So, the point is *reach out* and ask for help.

You'll be surprised what you can find!

Finally, remember to take your mentor's advice with a grain of salt. For example, if your mother suggests changing something, you can consider it. If a professor from an SLP program suggests something, you should *probably do it!* Ultimately you are responsible for your essays, and no one can guarantee that they will get you in.

SPEND TIME REVISING

When you have gotten to the point where your essay is about the right length and you think you have all the right ideas in place, spend time revising and polishing.

Look at the essay after ignoring it for a few days. Maybe even take a week or two between revisions. This will help you to look at it with fresh eyes each time.

Look for the following to revise:

- Clichés: Replace them with your own, original wording.
- Misspellings
- Confusing or overly complex sentences
- Using big words when simpler ones will work
- Punctuation
- Try to avoid abbreviations like *they're* and *I'm* if you can
- Shorten unnecessarily long sentences.
- Phrases that are repetitive

EMBRACE CHANGE (A.K.A. KILL YOUR DARLINGS)

One thing I struggle with when writing is getting attached to what I have written. I'll think to myself, "I have spent hours on this, and now I cannot change anything." Or, "Well this paragraph already says XYZ, so I can't get rid of it…" Or, "I love this sentence. How could I change it?"

Unfortunately, this mindset only prevents me from improving the essay. When I am finally willing to rewrite a paragraph or remove a whole section, that is when my writing improves the most.

Have you ever watched a DVD and on the "Extras" menu there are maybe a dozen deleted scenes? Film directors do the same thing- they may think something is critical, but later realize it is not so they leave it out. In the folder where I have my drafts saved, I also have 5 word documents each with a paragraph or two that I ended up cutting because it was not necessary, but I couldn't bear to delete *just in case*.

Don't be scared to delete or change, change, change. Trust the process.

FITTING THE ESSAY TO EACH SCHOOL

They say you should not use a cookie cutter personal statement that you send to each and every graduate school for speech language pathology. They're right...ish.

Your essay should *not* be the exact same for each school. But that doesn't mean you have to completely start over and write an original essay for each one. Even if you did, there would probably be a lot of overlap.

In this section, I am going to give you some tips and tricks on how to customize your personal statement for each school.

1. Research the Department You're Applying to!

In my interview with Treasyri (a practicing SLP and blogger: TheSpeechMentor), she described finding a graduate school like dating, and I think it is a great analogy.

Imagine you get one date to decide if you want to spend 2 years with someone. Scary, right? That is like a school offering admission to someone! Now imagine you're on that date and the person sitting across from you blurts out, "You're perfect for me. I've dreamed about you since I was in high school. I've always known I wanted to be with you." Do you believe any of it? No. So why would you use those same boring, hackneyed, empty phrases with a graduate school?

You need to research the school in mind and express why it is a good fit for you, and why you are a good fit for their program. Express those reasons clearly in your statement. Are they one of the few schools with a bilingual program? That's a perfect fit. Do they have a unique clinical rotation, like working with voice feminization? Is there a leading dysphagia or adult neurogenic researcher on the faculty? You should mention your overlapping research interests. It's okay if you're not sure yet. Speech pathology is a wide field. If you say you're interested in a specific area, you're not committing to anything yet.

Where do you find all of this info? Start on the department website. Read all of it. Most faculty have at least a brief paragraph describing their research interests on the department website; read them. Does the department have accounts on social media? Follow them! See what they post about.

If you can, get ahold of current students and ask them about their experience. What kind of stuff is emphasized across classes? What do the professors really care about? What is it like?

2. Know The University Too!

MOST graduate programs are pretty independent from the main university. You're often taking classes only within your department because the stuff you're learning is highly specialized. Even so, the wider university culture still influences the department you're in. Just like you researched the department, research the university.

Is it a liberal arts university? If yes, interdisciplinary studies will likely be highly valued. Can you incorporate that into your personal statement? If the university is a research institution, you should mention research in your essay. If the school is located in an urban area, your experiences growing up on a farm in a small town will seem unique. Is the university in an area with significant linguistic diversity?

The point is, try to get some idea of the culture of the institution and the context it exists within. Universities (as much as many might try to be) are not isolated from the communities in which they are located.

3. Drop a name or two.... And spell it right!

IF you've identified an area of interest (e.g., voice, child language, motor speech disorders, bilingualism, etc.), be sure to mention faculty you'd be interested in working with, by name! You could write something like, "I would love the opportunity to more closely observe Dr. Miller's research on melodic intonation therapy," or "It would be a privilege to study under Dr. Hernandez as he continues his research in quality of life measures in fluency disorders." These short statements go a long way to showing that you've done your research and you're picking the school for a reason, not simply because you're desperate.

If you are going to include this information, be *sure* about what you're saying. Don't guess at a professor's interests; make sure you've read their webpage, CV, or recall their name from an article. Speaking of which, it is an *excellent* idea to have read a few of their articles (at minimum the abstract) and have a basic understanding of their research.

Apart from mentioning specific faculty in your essay, mention the name of the university itself! You'd be surprised how many people don't. Oh, and be sure to spell the name right. Columbia and Colombia are not the same. Is it John Hopkins or Johns Hopkins? Seriously – triple check it.

CHAPTER 7

LETTERS OF RECOMMENDATION

Letters of recommendation (LOR) offer the admissions committee insight into you as an applicant from someone who can be more objective than you can. Ideally, these recommendations are coming from professors and instructors working in higher education.

You can think of LORs sort of like reviews on Amazon. Reviews give you insight into the positive and negative aspects of an item you're about to purchase. LORs help an admissions committee better understand the strengths and weaknesses of an applicant before they decide to invest thousands of dollars and years of training in them.

This chapter will cover the following:

- Who to ask?
- LOR Strategy: Playing the long game
- How to ask?
- After They Say Yes
- Frequently Asked Questions

Who to Ask

Knowing who to ask for a letter of recommendation can cause a real headache.

Who can I ask? How do I know? Is it better to ask A or B? So, who *can* you ask?

1. ASK: Whomever the school tells you to ask

Each school you apply to will specify how many LORs they require and also from whom the letters need to be. Most schools ask for three and specify that at least two of them must be from academic faculty (in other words: professors).

Read the guidelines from each university carefully and follow them! If they ask for two faculty in a related field, then the letters need to be from professors in Speech and Hearing Sciences or Communication Disorders. If you're not sure if a professor from linguistics class would count – call the program you're applying to and ask. Don't let your application be rejected for not following directions!

2. ASK: People you've built relationships with

Letter of Recommendation Golden Rule: Thou shalt visit a professor's office hours at least once before you ask for a letter.

You need to have a relationship with your LOR writer. If they know you (and especially if they like you) they'll write a much stronger letter.

Even if you're taking online classes, find a way to connect personally with your professors. Plan this out at the beginning of the semester ("I will visit each professor's office at least once during the first 3 weeks of class...") and then make it happen. It may be hard, but those visits will help you so much in the long run.

3. ASK: A strategic variety

WHAT seems better to you:

- Three letters of recommendation that all say, "Dionna is a great student" OR
- One letter that says "Dionna is a strong writer;" another "Dionna is attentive in class;" and finally "Dionna was a responsible student volunteer."

An assortment of letters that highlight a variety of skills and strengths is preferable to coming across one-dimensional.

Plan. Think about what each letter-writer can say about you. Did you write a strong paper for one professor? Maybe you gave a thorough presentation on a specific subject for another class. Can you ask someone who has observed you working with children or clients?

This is covered in more detail under *how to ask,* but when you do ask for the LOR, politely suggest what you think would make their LOR unique.

4. ASK: People who will write a strong LOR

THIS seems obvious but don't ask someone who won't (or can't) write a strong letter. You can discern this by asking: "I was wondering if you'd feel comfortable writing me a *positive* letter of recommendation for graduate school?" If the professor expresses some reservations, maybe they aren't your best option.

PLAY THE LONG GAME

Obtaining a strong letter of recommendation is much more than getting a good grade in a class and then asking the professor. To get the *best* letters of recommendation, you have to play the long game; it is a marathon not a sprint. That means you have to invest time (at least a semester but preferably at least two or three) and effort into truly impressing a professor, getting to know them, and showing that you're someone worth recommending strongly. And you are worth it!

So how do you do that?

Earn a good grade

An A is obviously recommended. Some (very picky) professors won't even consider writing a letter for someone who earned less than an A. However most professors are more than happy to write letters (and strong ones!) for someone who earned a B. So do your best to earn an A, but don't sweat it if you get a B.

Another important part of obtaining a strong letter of recommendation is attendance in class. If you don't go to class, how is a professor going to get to know you? You might be saying to yourself. *"But there are 80 people in the class— my professor doesn't even know who I am."* The thing is, they do notice who you are, even in a class of 80.

Make yourself known to the professor.

Attendance is only part of the battle. You should also ask questions, make comments, and actively participate in class. That's easy for extroverts and a lot harder for introverts.

If you dread raising your hand in class, make yourself known in other ways:

- Standout on assignments and tests.
- Stay after class to ask clarifying questions or comment on something you found interesting.
- Sit near the front and be attentive.
- Force yourself to raise your hand at least once per class, or once per week (if you prepare by doing all the reading before hand, this won't seem as daunting).
- Be early to class.

If these methods don't work for you, consider another amazing *and totally underutilized secret weapon of getting to know your professor: Office hours.* Go to office hours with questions, even if you have to make up the questions! Yes, you can make up questions: confirm things from class, ask if the professor can expand on a topic, ask about tips for where you can learn more.

Another way to make yourself know is to volunteer to help a professor with research or any projects they may be working on. If there isn't anything happening at the moment, try to find a moment to have a real conversation with the professor. Read some of their research and ask about it. Ask about their career path into the field. Ask for advice about looking at graduate programs. Just be sure to have at least one meaningful conversation with the professor before asking them for a recommendation.

All of this requires investing time and energy over an extended period of time. What if you have a professor one semester, but don't need your LOR until a year away? You worked hard in the class and cultivated a bit of a relationship. Maintain that relationship! Stop by their office hours next semester just to say hi. If something you're studying in another class reminds you of something you learned previously or is related, send a quick email saying, *"In SHS 450 we're learning about creating treatment plans and it reminded me of the assignment you gave us on selecting targets for articulation therapy in 428. Just wanted to take a moment to let you know and thank you again for such a good class last semester!"* Little points of random contact like that can go a long way to maintaining a relationship.

HOW TO ASK

If you've already developed a relationship with someone, asking for a letter of recommendation should be fairly straightforward. There are four key elements:

1. Ask in-person whenever possible.

Make an appointment with the person (or if they are a professor, you can drop by during office hours). It is okay to ask over the phone or via email only if an in-person visit is impossible. Why? LORs are all about personal relationships and if you don't feel comfortable asking in person, the relationship might not be strong enough.

2. Ask for a positive LOR.

Say something like, "Do you think you would be able to write me a strong, positive letter of recommendation?" Why is it important to include "strong" or "positive" in the question? Well, if a professor doesn't know you very well or thinks they can only write a lukewarm letter of recommendation, this is their chance for them to tell you. If a professor says anything less than, "Yes," consider asking someone else. If you have a LOR strategy, you can also politely and subtly incorporate it into your ask. For example, "I really enjoyed the paper I wrote in your class on how tongue height affects acoustic formants. Because of that class and my performance, I was wondering if you'd feel comfortable writing a strong, positive letter of recommendation."

3. Ask far in advance of the deadline.

The rule of thumb is at least one-month in advance of when the letter is due. Whenever possible, give as much time as possible. Many schools set their own deadlines to request LORs from faculty, otherwise they will be overwhelmed. Know if there is a policy in your department and plan ahead.

4. Provide a recommender packet.

Many professors will ask for these things automatically, but if they don't you should provide the following:

- A copy of your CV/Resume

- A copy of the current draft of your personal statement (it doesn't have to be finished)

- An unofficial transcript

- A list of the schools the letters are being sent to AND instructions on how to submit them

AFTER THEY SAY YES

Before you leave their office, you may want to ask some important questions. The purpose of these questions is to make your life and the recommender's life easier. Some things you might want to know include:

- I'd like to give you a copy of my CV and personal statement in case they help. Would you prefer them by email or paper copies?

- Do you need anything else from me to help support your writing these letters?

- I know you're very busy; when would it be okay for me to check in with you about the letter? Can we set a date a few weeks ahead of the deadline, so I'm able to keep track of my applications but also not pester you with emails?

> A Word on Harmful Letters:
>
> Chapter 8 will cover egregious mistakes you should avoid making in regards to personal statements and letters of recommendation. Be sure to read it carefully.

That last question is critical. It helps you help the professor by knowing when to reach out without annoying them.

Finally, once a person agrees to write you a positive letter of recommendation you should thank them sincerely. It is always a good idea to send a simple, personalized thank you note. Gifts (even small ones) are generally not appropriate. As health care professionals, SLP's have strict and necessary ethical standards regarding potential conflicts of interest.

FAQ: Can I Ask...

Despite the above tips and tricks, I'm sure you still have questions about asking specific people in your life. Here are some of the most common people that students usually wonder about asking...

My priest / preacher / rabbi / faith leader:

THE SHORT ANSWER: YES

The long answer: Assuming the person meets the above mentioned standards, you just have to make sure the letter will focus on academic and professional strengths that will help you in grad school. You don't necessarily need a character letter explaining you're a good person; you need a letter explaining you'd be a strong student and good future clinician.

The family I babysit for:

THE SHORT ANSWER: YES

The long answer: If this person is a strong writer and you have a relationship, this can be a great person to speak well to your abilities as a future clinician and maybe your time management skills. However, this may not be the best source if this person is also a family member or close personal friend. If that is the case, tread carefully.

My boss at _____ :

THE SHORT ANSWER: YES

The long answer: Employers look at things differently than the way professors do. If you're going to ask a boss / supervisor for a letter of recommendation, make sure it is detailed enough and focuses on things that matter for grad school (time management, teamwork, ability to receive criticism, critical thinking, etc) rather than things employers might focus on (punctuality, company loyalty, etc).

My family member who is also a _____:

THE SHORT ANSWER: NO

The long answer: No. Relatives or family members should never write an LOR on your behalf for graduate school. It is biased and therefore meaningless to the committee.

Can I ask a professor even though I earned a B in her class?

THE SHORT ANSWER: YES

The longer answer: If that professor is willing to write strong, positive letter, then the grade doesn't matter.

Can I ask a professor who I did research with but didn't take a class with?

THE SHORT ANSWER: YES!

The longer answer: Yes! Research experience is invaluable to an application.

Can I ask someone who I haven't worked with in a long time?

THE SHORT ANSWER: IT DEPENDS

The long answer: If this person will still remember you and be able to write a strong letter, than absolutely. If it has been a very long time, consider a visit or at least a phone call to re-establish the relationship.

I was a teacher / educational assistant / or some other professional in a related field, can I ask my supervisor?

THE SHORT ANSWER: YES

The long answer: If the person is going to write about your readiness for graduate school, then yes! Also, make sure that this is only 1 of your 3 letters of recommendation. The majority need to be from academic references. My department chair (aka supervisor) when I was a teacher wrote me a wonderful letter of recommendation that surely helped me get into graduate school.

Can I ask a professor from another area like psychology or business?

THE SHORT ANSWER: YES

The long answer: If you majored in SHS (or something similar), then you could get 1 LOR from a related field (Linguistics, Psychology, Education, etc.) but it is best to try for SHS faculty. If you're an "out of fielder" (like I was!) then you can definitely use professors from other disciplines. Again it is best if they're from a related field, but is not necessary. For the definitive answer on this, be sure to call the program you're interested in, speak with the graduate advisor, explain your situation (briefly), and ask for clarification.

CHAPTER 8

KISSES OF DEATH

Some mistakes can be overlooked in the graduate school application process; some mistakes are serious enough that they can be considered *a kiss of death* to your application.

This chapter is based on research done by Dr. Drew C. Appleby and Dr. Karen M. Appleby. In one of their studies, they sent a letter to the *Chair of the Graduate Admissions Committee* at 457 different institutions. The letter explained the study and asked the respondent to give examples of a "Kiss of Death" that might occur in an application. The letter defines a *Kiss of Death* as, "aberrant types of information that cause graduate admissions committees to reject otherwise strong applicants." While their research was regarding graduate admissions in psychology, many of the same lessons apply to the field of speech-language pathology as well.

88 chairpersons responded to the survey providing a wealth of information about potential pitfalls and atrocious mistakes that may disqualify strong applicants. In those 88 responses, there were 156 examples of *Kisses of Death* (KOD's). After analyzing the responses, five major KOD categories were created and are summarized for your benefit below.

KOD 1. Damaging Personal Statements

After your GRE and GPA get your application through the first filter and onto the committee's radar, your personal statement is the most important part of standing out and making a good impression. It is the perfect way to inform the admissions committee about you, your goals, background, and professional trajectory.

Calling it the "Personal Statement" might be misleading because it shouldn't be "too personal." In fact, the study reports that "damaging personal statements" are one of the main Kisses of Death in the grad school application process. There are four types of damaging personal statements identified in the survey:

Damaging Personal Statement: Personal Mental Health

Examples of this particular KOD include "emotional instability" or "evidence of untreated mental illness." Let me clarify something: It is okay to have suffered mental illness (pretty much everyone has at some point), but *untreated* illness (or the possibility of it) could be viewed negatively during the admissions process.

The article mentions that admissions committees are strongly put off "when students highlight how they were drawn to graduate study because of significant personal problems or trauma. Graduate school is an academic/career path, not a personal treatment or intervention for problems." I think that last sentence is worth repeating: " *Graduate school is an academic/career path, not a personal treatment or intervention for problems.*"

Personally, *I think* it's okay to mention if you received speech or language therapy at any point in your life. It can be a great way to introduce how you came to know the field. However, I think it would be unprofessional to say you want to earn a degree in SLP for self-treatment or something to that effect. A personal example, I speak Spanish and am married to a Mexican (who speaks four languages).

My children will be multilingual which *strongly* relates to my interest in bilingual language development, but I didn't mention that *anywhere* in my application materials because it crosses the line from professional interest into personal.

Damaging Personal Statement: Excessive Altruism

IF you are applying to attend school in Speech Language Pathology, it's obvious that you are interested in helping people. Don't waste too much time reinforcing something so obvious. The original article calls this Kiss of Death *"excessive altruism."*

Furthermore, statements such as "I want to help everyone;" or "I think I am a strong candidate because people view me as warm, empathetic, and caring;" will not impress an admissions committee. Flattering words regarding your personal character are better left to your recommenders.

Instead of focusing on altruism, focus on things like your research interests, academic strengths, and professional experiences. Your personal motives for entering the field are valuable, but they can easily work against you. Becoming an SLP is first and foremost a professional endeavor. Therefore it should be approached with professionalism.

Damaging Personal Statement: Excessive Self Disclosure

SPEECH-LANGUAGE Pathologists teach people social skills (among many other things), so they must be adept at measuring boundaries and using interpersonal skills. "Excessive self-disclosure" is the 3rd subcategory of "Damaging Personal Statements" discussed by the Applebys in their article.

An example given in the article of this KOD is the telling of a "long saga about how the student had finished school despite incredible odds." This kind of story might be interesting to the committee if it's told in a professional (not self-victimizing) way that is also brief. It is such a sensitive topic that it must be handled carefully. You don't want the admissions committee to perceive you as "making excuses" for any shortcomings in your personal narrative.

If you have something that helps contextualize a bad semester or a failed class, you first want to consider if it is worth addressing. Personal example: I failed and had to retake a finance class when I was an undergraduate student. I came up with a pretty good, introspective explanation about why I'd failed the class. It was 153 words long. When I really thought about it though, I realized it was not worth drawing the committee's attention to a Corporate Finance class which probably didn't receive anything more than a cursory glance. Further, it would have been almost one third of a page of my personal statement. If you think an issue is worth addressing, do it briefly— you don't want to use too much of your valuable SOP space.

Other common situations that people struggle with are the death of a loved one, an accident, or suffering a blow to your health. These could all be valid to include in a personal statement, but it must be done with professionalism. In these cases, it's best to seek advice from an admissions expert or professor.

Damaging Personal Statement: Professionally Inappropriate

Aᴛ first I was surprised that the Applebys article even listed "professionally inappropriate!" Then I read some of the examples given in the article. One applicant wrote about their performance in pornographic movies. Another turned her SOP into a lengthy allegory in which she was Dorothy on the yellow-brick road to graduate school. Neither of these were well received by the admissions committee (as you can imagine).

Anything that is excessively cutesy or clever is probably a bad idea (i.e., if Elle Woods from Legally Blonde would do it, you probably don't want to). At some point, you might be tempted to include jokes or humor in your essays. I was certainly tempted to lighten the mood of my essays, but I know that these things can easily be misunderstood or missed completely. It is best to avoid attempts at humor.

Excessive religious references should also be avoided. The Dean of one Graduate program quoted in the article said, "Being religious is OK, but it has little relevance to research... or graduate school."

KOD 2. HARMFUL LETTERS OF RECOMMENDATION

Letters of Recommendation (LORs) are the best way an admissions committee can learn about you apart from your personal statement. Because they're ideally written by peers of the admission committee, they might even be more valuable than the SOP.

If an LOR is poorly written, it can be a Kiss of Death. The Applebys divided this KOD into 2 categories.

Harmful LOR 1 of 2: Undesirable applicant characteristics

CERTAIN characteristics are required for success in graduate school: Determination, intelligence, motivation, independence, responsibility, the ability to work with others. Letters of recommendation often reference these personal traits, and so any LOR that doesn't include these things is going to hurt your application. The original article included several examples of KOD statements in letters like, "arrogant and not a team player," "unreliable" and "immature."

To avoid recommenders writing things like this in your letter, remember: make sure that you have a good relationship with the person before you ask for an LOR! Also, *always* ask someone if they can write a *positive* letter of recommendation.

Harmful LOR 2 of 2: Inappropriate Sources

JUST because someone is going to say nice things about you doesn't mean they'd be a good recommender. The admissions committee will consider the source of the letter and their relationship to you. If the source is inappropriate, it is a Kiss of Death for your application.

Some examples of inappropriate sources (that people have actually used):

- Parents
- Family / Relatives
- Employees
- Your therapist
- Travel agents
- Boyfriends or girlfriends
- Yourself

KOD 3. LACK OF INFORMATION ABOUT A PROGRAM

During my conversation with Treasyri (a practicing SLP), she often used the analogy that finding a graduate school is like finding a boyfriend/girlfriend. Imagine hearing this on a first date, "You're perfect for me. I want to marry you!" You do *not* want your personal statement to be like that. You can't just jump right in and say, "We're made for each other," and you can't spend the whole statement talking about yourself (just like on a first date!)

In your application you have to make the school think they're ready to marry you after the first date (or at least invite you on a second date... a.k.a. an interview). And you do that by showing them you understand who they are (program focus) and you have reasons to show why you should be together (your fit).

Lack of Info: Program Focus

It is imperative that you understand the focus of any program you're applying to. As you know, Masters in speech-language pathology that lead to clinical certification (CCC), are pretty tightly regulated and might not have much wiggle room. But professors definitely have their own research interests, preferred populations, and areas of expertise. You should absolutely study the research interests of these professors and even read some of their publications! You should be able to articulate how your interests align with those of the faculty at the school you're applying to.

Not understanding the specific focus of a program sends the message that you're desperate and willing to go anywhere (even if you are, you don't want the admissions committee to know that). Your interests might not align 100%, but you do want to know what your getting yourself into, and programs want that too!

Imagine if a school invests in you and invites you to their program. When it comes time for your first clinical rotation, you find out that you have a pretty slim chance of ever working in a hospital, which is your career goal. You're going to be pretty frustrated, and so is the school!

Lack of Info: Fit Into the Program

AFTER you know the focus of the program, you should be able to demonstrate how you fit into it!

You don't have to have 100%, laser-focused interests. I didn't when I applied! I knew I was interested in "bilingualism," and that was about it. The area of bilingualism is huge and links to every other topic in the field. But I researched programs with that specialty and within those programs I researched faculty with that specialty. I read (a tiny fraction) of their research and even scheduled phone interviews to learn more.

Here's an example of a bad fit: The program you're applying to has mostly faculty who have done research and work with geriatric populations. If your personal statement is filled with your passion for children and helping them succeed in school, it is less likely to grab the attention of the committee.

One respondent to the survey by the Applebys said, *"I'm very attentive to whether a students' interest match our training. I expect a statement of personal interest that displays a convincing, compelling desire for what we have to offer from its start to finish. It's a kiss of death when I read a personal essay that describes an applicant's life-long goal of serving humankind and has a paragraph tacked on to the end that "personalizes" the essay for that particular school..."*

The take-away lesson for me is that you cannot use a generic statement like, "The _____ University is the perfect place for me," without backing it up with clear evidence and examples.

KOD 4. POOR WRITING SKILLS

You should have learned how to write while completing your undergraduate degree. Your application to graduate school (be it a writing sample, personal statement, or simply correspondence with the department) is not a chance to practice. It is the moment to put your best foot forward.

Poor Writing Skills: Spelling and grammatical errors

SPELLING and grammar mistakes should not happen in any part of your application. They are immediate KODs for many committee members. I think an errant comma might be overlooked, but have someone (or several "someones") read your application materials before sending them. Don't risk sending in an application with errors for the sake of time.

Triple check the spelling of names of professors and institutions mentioned.

Poor Writing Skills: Poor Writing

IN addition to the mechanics of writing, the craft is also key. Style and structure are important in graduate study because you could easily become a representative for your institution or professors through your writing. The main writing sample you're going to submit is the personal statement. Be sure it has a definite structure and strong content. One of the people surveyed for the research replied that a KOD is "overly long and detailed statements of purpose that are poorly edited."

KOD 5. MISFIRED ATTEMPTS TO IMPRESS

To me, the most entertaining part of the Applebys research article was the section on Misfired Attempts to Impress. It was divided into two main ideas:

Criticism of an undergraduate program AND/ OR unsupported praise for the institution

THIS sounds like: "I didn't learn enough in undergrad which is why I want to earn a masters at your amazing institution." One respondent to the Applebys' survey said, "The candidate will give a very bad impression if he/she blames others for his/her poor academic record. Example: Faculty here at X university were unwilling to help me succeed."

In general, you should avoid any sort of negativity in your personal statement or application in general. Remember, the admissions committee is picking their future students, coworkers, and peers.

Name dropping

MENTIONING an important family member's work in the field without any substantial professional connection does not build your case as an applicant. Also, don't seek letters from high-profile recommenders without a clear reason to do so. One candidate mentioned in the article obtained an LOR from a senator who was a family friend. The letter commented little on the applicant and much more on the senator's career and power.

Be sure that any connections to famous people are substantiated and professional, just like they should be for *any* letter of recommendation.

WHAT IT ALL MEANS

These *Kisses of Death* can all be avoided by exhibiting professionalism, understanding the formal nature of admissions process, and grasping the culture of graduate education. If you have already started the application process, be sure to skim over your materials for any signs of the *Kisses of Death!*

Taking time now to properly vet your application could help you avoid an automatic disqualification later.

CHAPTER 9

INTERVIEWS

THE BASICS

Interviews in the graduate school admissions process are a way for schools to meet the "real you."

If you've ever done online dating, you know exactly why this is important. The person's profile sounds perfect, like it was written especially for you. Their profile picture shows perfect hair and a gorgeous smile. You message each other jokes and well-timed flirty comments. You find yourself day-dreaming about how you'll spend the rest of your life with this person. Then you meet for the first date, and it is a huge let down. Even if the person was 100% sincere in everything they wrote, it's different to meet them in-person and see how you two click.

Interviews for graduate school are similar. The committee wants to make sure you are as amazing a candidate in-person (or over the phone) as on paper.

Do all schools do interviews?

No.

Interviews are costly and time-consuming. Therefore, many programs do not use them. Some universities even argue that there is an ethical advantage to *not* doing interviews, as committee members are less likely to be biased about race, sex, accent, or other potential points of discrimination.

Is there a difference between a visit day and an interview?

Yᴇs...ᴍᴀʏʙᴇ.

An interview is a more formal evaluation than a visit day. But if you have a visit day, you can bet you will be judged, measured, and evaluated as a candidate, even if it's done informally. Some schools may conduct interviews while hosting a visit day. If that is the case, you'll be told that you're going to be interviewed. If not, you should still prepare and present the best you that you can for the visit day. Even if there is no formal interview, it is still your best chance to make a good impression on the faculty.

Pʀᴇᴘᴀʀɪɴɢ ꜰᴏʀ ᴛʜᴇ Iɴᴛᴇʀᴠɪᴇᴡ

There are a few things you'll need to know to prepare properly for the interview. You may have to do some detective work to find these things out. Try contacting the person scheduling the interviews or the chair of the admissions committee to ask. Be prepared, they might not have all the answers, and that is okay too.

1. Is it an open or closed file interview?

Aɴ *open file* interview is when the interviewer(s) has access to your application and can make reference to it. They have typically read your essays and seen your transcripts before speaking with you.

A *closed file* interview is when the interviewer(s) has *not* seen your application and probably only knows your name. You'll have to start from square one and assume they know nothing about you.

2. Is it in-person, on-the-phone, or a video call?

THIS is something that will probably be explained when they're setting up the interview. The medium will definitely make a difference in how you practice and perform.

3. How long is it scheduled for?

YOU need to be prepared to adjust your answers appropriately based on the time you have. If the interview is 15 minutes, practice with that amount of time to get a feel for it. Ask when you're contacted to schedule a date and time.

4. How many interviewers and how many interviewees?

THE most frequent format of interviews is 2 interviewers (usually faculty or clinical instructors) and 1 candidate. Some programs do things differently though like group interviews, 1-on-1, or any number of other options. Ask about the format in advance.

HOW TO PREPARE

YOU wouldn't send the first draft of your personal statement directly to the admissions committee, would you? Of course not. You've reviewed it. Edited it. Changed it. And (hopefully) asked several others to do the same. In the same way, you should definitely practice for your interview.

Mock interviews are your best bet for practicing.

IF you are still a currently enrolled student, *definitely* go to your university's career center (or equivalent) and see if they offer practice interviews. Many universities offer mock interviews with your peers (who are trained in this sort of thing), which is a great preparation tool. If that is not available to you, check out the **S**ervice **C**ore **of** **R**etired **E**xecutives (SCORE), which is an organization of former business executives who offer all kinds of great mentoring services, including mock interviews. They have chapters across the U.S.

If those other options don't work for you, don't fret! Just ask a friend. Set it up and take it seriously. You should both dress up and find a professional-ish space to use (or at least some place where you'll feel out of your comfort zone).

With any practice interview, try using a tablet or phone to record yourself. Yes, it is *quite* uncomfortable to watch and listen to yourself, but it will help you become aware of any awkward stress responses (like playing with your hair or holding onto the chair with a white-knuckled-death-grip), and it will drastically increase your confidence for the real thing.

Practice Questions

You should probably go over some practice questions before your mock interview and most definitely before the real thing. Think of your own. Google it. Or skip to the end of this chapter for some common questions used in interviews.

How to Answer Tough Questions

The first thing you should do is practice your responses. Important note, the point here is *not* to have memorized responses – these will be easily spotted and will make you look like a nervous robot. Remember, SLPs are experts at analyzing language and communication. The purpose of practicing is to get comfortable talking about yourself and being mentally prepared with your strongest talking points.

It is very possible that you'll get a "behavioral" question during your interview. These are questions like *"Tell us about a time..."* or *"Describe a situation in which..."* Using behavioral questions, the interviewers consider your past behavior as a predictor of future behavior. What you should try to do is give specific examples that illustrate the characteristics you think they're looking for.

For example:

- Tell us about a time you had to work with a difficult client or parent.

- Tell us about a time you had to take on a large responsibility.

- Tell me about a time you had to be very flexible to accomplish your goal.

A nifty "tool" to help you answer these types of questions is the *S.T.A.R. method*. I learned about it when I worked as a Peer Career Assistant and Mock Interviewer at Truman State University's Career Center.

- **S** stands for "Situation:" Describe the context and set the scene.

- **T** is for "Task:" Describe what you needed to get done.

- **A** is for "Action:" Describe what you did in order to complete the task.

- **R** is the "Result:" This step is often forgotten by interviewees. Talk about what happened! The result doesn't have to be positive (although if it isn't, be sure to explain what you learned from the failure).

How does this work in reality? Imagine you're asked: "Tell us about a time you had to change your plans quickly to meet a deadline or goal."

S: Well, I was teaching 6th grade English at the time.

T: My students needed to be at a certain point in the novel we were reading as a class but because of several cancelled school days, we were behind. So, we're in our last class that week, and we're about to get started when the fire alarms go off.

A: We evacuated the classroom and went to the soccer field to wait for instructions. As soon as we got to the field, I sat my class down and kept reading the novel to them. I told them we would work on their listening comprehension skills.

R: The technique worked to keep them calm during the drill. The principal actually congratulated me on how well behaved they were! We were able to catch up on our work despite the surprise fire drill. And as an added bonus, my students got extra practice with listening skills.

See how the STAR method gets you through the major points of answering the question quickly and easily? The *result* is the part people most often forget, so be sure not to let that happen to you.

You Need to Have Questions for The Interviewers (even if you don't get to ask them)

THIS is your chance to find out specific information about the program and/or show that you've done your research.

- Don't ask for information that is easily available on the department's website (which you should have read before the interview). You will seem unprepared.

- Do ask for *further* information about specific programs. For example, let's say the department has a study abroad program. Asking about it shows that 1) You've done your research about the department's offerings and 2) It sets you apart because of your interest.

- Do ask about clinical rotations and supervision if it's not well explained on the website.

- Do ask about assistantships and financial aid if you're interested.

WHAT TO WEAR

Dressing professionally is important for a graduate school interview regardless of the format.

Why?

If you're going to an in-person interview, you should definitely dress up. You'll project maturity and professionalism. Think about it from the perspective of the interviewers: not only are they selecting future students, they are deciding which candidates will be working in hospitals, schools, and other settings which require the highest of ethical and professional standards. Does your dress prove you can handle the responsibility?

If you are doing a phone interview where you won't be seen, you should still consider dressing up. Believe it or not, how you dress affects how you act. Even though the interviewers won't see you, they'll hear the difference it makes in how you speak and answer questions.

Dress Code Tips for Women

- Suit & hosiery: Preferably in navy, grey or black
- A skirt-suit is generally viewed more favorably than a pantsuit
- Keep your hair away from your face (so they can see you!)
- Minimal jewelry
- Closed-toe shoes
- Tattoos covered
- No perfume or fragrances: you never know who is allergic to what or what someone might not like
- No unusual piercings

Dress Code Tips for Men

- Matched suit: Preferably in navy, grey or black with a traditional tie
- A short, professional hair cut; clean shaved or well-kept beard

- Wedding ring and/or watch
- Clean, shined shoes and matching belt
- Tattoos covered
- No perfume or fragrances: you never know who is allergic to what or what someone might not like (especially true for medical placements)
- No unusual piercings

A note on dress code: These gender-binary-role-affirming recommendations do not reflect what should or should not be standards of professionals and grooming. Instead, they reflect the most conservative options to hopefully maximice your first impression and chances for admission.

Is it possible to overdress?

It's almost impossible to overdress. In several years serving on the selection committee for a prestigious international scholarship, I have not once thought, "That candidate is overdressed." On the other hand, I distinctly remember a few candidates (who I did not recommend) who dressed too casually; I can assure you that I was not the only committee member who noticed that they were undressed. Is it an official part of the decision making process? No. Does it affect my perception of the candidate? Yes. Does that seep into the comments I leave on the evaluation form? Yes. Does it subconsciously affect whether I rank the candidate as a four or five on different criteria? Yes.

An example: We were conducting a video call interview for a young man living in Perú. He was dressed in a full suit and tie. He was also visibly sweating. As we were wrapping up the interview, one of the panelists made a comment to lighten the mood – "Are you sweating because you're nervous or because of the heat?" The candidate answered that it was sweltering hot but that he wanted to make a good impression. I cannot honestly say for sure if that small, offhand comment which plays no official part in the selection process made a difference in each committee member's decision; However, I can say that the committee pleasantly discussed how we had perceived him to be committed, polite, and a strong candidate. And I can say that the young man was awarded the fellowship.

Phone & Teleconference Interviews

If your interview is over the phone or via video, there are some special considerations to keep in mind.

Quiet Place:

For either medium, it is *very* important that you find a quiet place to conduct the interview. You don't want loud noise in the background, constant interruptions, dogs barking, etc. Distractions waste time and frustrate the interviewers.

> One candidate I interviewed for a scholarship conducted her interview in a cyber cafe. Unfortunately, there were teenage boys in the background loudly playing a videogame. She probably had few options for a reliable Internet connection, but the distracting background noise made it impossible to hear her responses. It was an unfortunate circumstance that we didn't have time to correct; on paper she was a stellar candidate.

Dress Up:

If you're being interviewed via videocall, you'll be visible over the camera. Dress just as you would for an in-person interview. *Even if the interview is audio only (like over the phone) you should still dress up, as previously discussed.*

Avoid Verbal Fillers:

IF you are the type of person who uses many feedback cues such as "Yes," or "Okay," during conversation, you'll need to cut those out. They can be very distracting over the phone or on Skype. The interviewer might think you're interrupting.

Here are some important technical considerations:

Ethernet connection:

You should get an ethernet cable and plug directly into the router rather than using Wi-Fi. The connection is faster and more stable. You might think you have fast Wi-Fi, but do you want to test it during an interview? Connection problems where your voice fades in and out and can easily frustrate the committee. Unfortunately, they don't have the time to wait for you to reconnect or repeat each of your answers through fade-outs and static.

Headphones and microphone:

USE a pair of headphones preferably with a microphone. The small earbuds that come with an iPhone or Apple computer are great and almost universally compatible. They make it easier for you and the interviewers to hear each other.

Professional/Neutral Background:

IF you're on camera, it is not only important that you're well-dressed, but that the background behind you is neutral or professional: plain walls, no flashy colors or posters, good lighting, etc. You don't have to be somewhere fancy, just somewhere neutral. Take the time to plan this beforehand.

A candidate I interviewed sat on the edge of her unmade bed in jeans and a low cut t-shirt. There was dirty laundry spread about the bed behind her. Immediately after the call, all of the committee members asked if each other if they thought she had just rolled out of bed for the interview! That's NOT the impression you want to make.

PRO-TIPS TO STEP-UP YOUR GAME

Connect with Interviewers: Apart from wanting to impress the interviewers with your well-thought-out and critical responses, you want to find a way to connect with them as people and professionals. Listen for something that you can use to link your interests and experiences with those of the interviewers. It is best not to be contrived and insincere. If you genuinely express yourself, something will most likely come up.

Skills to Mention: There are certain skills that faculty look for in prospective students because they'll be necessary for success as clinicians. ASHA put out a report about the changing needs of SLP and Audiology students in the new century. The article is worth a read – especially the section called *Nine Workplace Success Skills Graduate Students Need to Learn*. I've copied out these nine skills for you below, but be sure to read the actual article for more info on each one.

1. Planning and priority setting

2. Organizing and time management

3. Managing diversity

4. Team building

5. Interpersonal savvy and peer relationships

6. Organizational agility

7. Conflict management

8. Problem solving, perspective, and creativity

9. Dealing with paradox and learning on the fly

Another useful document is ASHA's 2010 report on trends in the profession. Many of the trends won't help you out in the interview, but there are a few worth working into your responses such as…

1. **A Diverse Future:** This section of the report discusses increasing diversity of all types; "cultural competence" among clinicians is increasingly important. Socioeconomic, racial, national, sexual orientation, linguistic, regional, etc. are examples of factors that contribute to cultural competence.

2. **Technology Marches Forward:** This section discusses issues like online education, telepractice, virtual clinical experiences, and innovation.

3. **Clinical Population Outlook:** This section basically discusses the fact that the average age of the population is rising and that they will need services.

Research the School: This should be pretty obvious, but learn *everything you possible can* about the department *and* university before the interview. Look for key objectives that appear in multiple places on the website. These are part of ongoing institutional dialog. Using certain "key words" and "buzz words" can subtly indicate you're a part of that dialog. Note you should *not* memorize the department's key objectives and try to pass them off as your life goals (that would be silly and transparent butt-kissing), but if you use the similar language, it could have a subtle influence how the interviewers perceive your responses.

Work the Waiting Room: If your interview is in-person, the interview starts the moment you step on campus! Always be extremely polite to anyone you interact with, especially departmental secretaries or other office workers. You have no idea the power they can wield over your application. If you're in a waiting room with other candidates, be friendly and make small talk. If there are any current students around, talk with them. Anyone you meet could give feedback about you and your application.

FOLLOW UP

How you handle yourself after the interview is almost as important as how you handle yourself during the interview. In other words, you *need to write a thank you note.*

During your interview, be sure to get the names of all of the interviewers you interact with, and key topics they mention. Then you can personalize your thank you note to each person. Your note should be something simple and professional (nothing flashy or over the top). You can use nice stationary or buy blank notes.

Absolutely *do not* do something like sending flowers, chocolates, or any other "gift" beyond a simple thank you note. Far from impressing the committee, you might make them think you are desperate, unable to measure professional boundaries, or even trying to bribe them. Remember when we compared this process to dating? Don't come across too strong!

If the interview was via phone, consider emailing your thank-you notes. I suggest emailing them to the department office for distribution unless professors specifically provided you their emails during the interview.

As for what to write, that's simple: Thank you!

- Be sure to address the person by name and title for example: Dr. Blaker or Professor Hanson.
- Express your thanks for their time
- Mention a connection you might have made during the interview

Thank you Example One

Professor Blaker,

Thank you very much for taking the time to speak with me regarding my application. I appreciate that personalized element to the process. Moreover, I was pleasantly surprised to learn that you are also interested in accent modification! It would be a pleasure to learn from you about that topic and others.

With gratitude,

Your name

Thank you Example Two:

Ms. Hanson,

I would like to express my sincere thanks for your taking the time to speak with me. I am impressed by the personalized and thorough admissions process at UNM. I hope to have the opportunity to learn with you, especially how to work with bilingual, Spanish-English speaking clients.

Sincerely,

Your Name

Keep thank-you notes short and sweet. You don't want to waste the person's time or appear sly / scheming by using it as a second-chance to talk endlessly about yourself.

Also, be sure to send a thank you note to the secretary or program administrator who helped you schedule the interview! This person is often overlooked by applicants but is very close to the faculty.

Try to send thank you notes a day or two after the interview.

Don't be a Pest

AFTER the interview you're going to be *even more anxious* to know the results of the admission process. Be patient! Don't contact the program administrator repeatedly. They receive myriad requests—don't make it worse and slow them down. Just try to be patient.

COMMON INTERVIEW QUESTIONS

You absolutely cannot anticipate all of the questions you may be asked during your interview. Here are some of the most common questions across interviews and some suggestions for structuring your answer.

WARNING: Do *not* memorize responses to these questions or any others. You'll come across like a robot! What you actually need to do with practice is get comfortable thinking quickly and speaking about yourself.

1. Tell us about yourself

THIS is a common starter question. You should *definitely* expect it or a variation of it. It's not a trick question; the interviewer is just looking to get to know you on a personal level and also help you get comfortable starting the interview. I recommend a simple past, present, future approach to this question: This where I'm from... this is what I'm doing now...and this is where I'm going.

> Example answer: Well, I'm from a small town in the midwest. I went to undergrad at a public liberal arts school, and that's when I first found out about SLP. Currently I'm working as an ESL teacher at a middle school and really enjoying getting to apply my skills. But I know I want to go back to grad school and eventually start working as an SLP. I

think I'm interested in school-age populations, but honestly adult aphasia sounds really interesting too, and I know UNM has strong faculty in both areas.

2. Why do you want to become an SLP?

This the *fundamental question* of the interview. It may come in different forms: What drew you to the field of SLP? How did you discover the field? What are your reasons for applying? etc. Your answer will probably mirror your personal statement.

3. Have you identified any areas of interest in the field?

This is a great question that serves a few purposes. For the interviewers, it helps them find out how well you might fit into their program. For example if you say, "Oh I definitely want to work with adult neurogenic disorders," and the school doesn't have a specialist in that area it might be a tough sell. So this is an *opportunity* for you to show you've researched the program. You could say, "Oh I really am interested in working with adult voice disorders. I know your faculty member Dr. Youngyeun is doing some research on treatment in that area."

What do you say if you *don't* have any areas of interest? That's perfectly fine, just word it in the right way. Instead of: "No…I don't have any specific interests yet." Say, "Well, one thing I like about the field of SLP is the variety. I don't have any one area of interest yet, and I'm excited about grad school at_____University because I know I'll be exposed to lots of areas like_____with professor so-and-so and_____."

4. How do you manage your time?

They are asking this question because graduate school demands excellent time management skills. During several semesters, you will not only be a full-time student, but also a clinician with a caseload of clients to provide therapy to, reports to write, and sessions to plan. This doesn't even take into account the myriad things in your personal life. Your answer should honestly explain what tools you use to keep yourself organized. If you have time you might share a quick story about a time when you were particularly busy and how you met deadlines.

5. How do you handle stress?

THIS is directly related to the time-management question. Life is stressful. Throw graduate school into the mix *and* being a student-clinician…you're in for a bumpy ride. The interviewer wants to know that when you have a big project due, a take-home exam coming up, and two therapy plans due you're not going to drop out of school. Your answer should just explain some of the techniques you use for stress relief (exercise, meditation, talking it out with friends, regularly scheduled movie nights). If you have time, you might share a quick anecdote about how you learned the importance of stress management.

6.Do you have any research experience? If so, tell us about it.

IF you have research experience, talk about what you did. Even if you did something relatively small for a big project, that's acceptable. The tricky part is when you don't have research experience. First, re-assess your academic work. Think about a project you did during class. Did you have to read articles and journals to write an essay? That's research. If you absolutely cannot think of any research experience, simply say: "I haven't had the opportunity yet to get involved with much research." If you *are* interested in learning more about research, say so!

7. What interested you in this University?

This question tests how well you did your research on the school. You should have some detailed answers prepared. Maybe you're interested in a study abroad program they have. Maybe you like their focus on medical SLP. Is this program known for a focus on diversity that really matters to you? Maybe there is a specific professor you're interested in.

What do you do if you're applying to a school because it's your only option in a geographic area and you can't move, for whatever reason? That's a tough situation to address. I'd recommend you research the school and the program enough that you find something about the program that excites you. Additionally, for one reason or another, you're committed to staying in your local community. Chances are the university is too— find a way to weave that commitment into your answer.

Here is a list of other common interview questions. You might think about how you would answer each of these, but remember: do not memorize any preset answers.

General Questions

- What is your background and why are you interested in becoming an SLP?
- Why are you interested in our program/University?
- What do you look for in a supervisor?
- How do you handle criticism?
- Tell us about an academic challenge and how you dealt with it.
- Why do you think you should be admitted over other applicants?
- You may have classes from 8am to 8pm with student meetings running even later. How will you handle this serious time commitment?

- What did you learn from_____experience that you listed on your resume?

SLP-Related Questions

- We know you're not an SLP yet, but what do you think is the most frustrating or challenging part of this field? What about the most rewarding?

- As a future SLP, what do you think are the elements of an effective therapy plan?

- Have you identified any areas of interest within the field?

- Do you have any special skills or certifications that could be relevant to the field? (For example, speaking a foreign language, teaching license, etc.)

- In the program, you'll be interacting with lots of different people from various backgrounds and ages. What kind of social/practical skills do you bring with you?

Curve-Ball Questions

- How likely are you to attend our university if we offer you admission?

- If you were a kitchen utensil, what would you be and why? (I was seriously asked this during a scholarship interview.)

- If you were trapped on a deserted island, what three objects would you want with you and why?

- What's the last book you read for fun?

Some Questions YOU may ask the interviewers

- What is your favorite part about working in this program?
- What do you think is the biggest advantage of attending this University instead of other programs?
- How are mentoring relationships established, formally or informally?
- What opportunities are there to get involved in research?
- What types of clinical placements are available? (Only ask this question if the answer isn't clear on the website)

CHAPTER 10

THE GRE

You're probably hoping to read some magical words like *don't worry about the GRE* or *your scores don't really matter*. But let's be honest: your GRE scores do matter, and you do need to prepare for the exam.

WHAT IS THE GRE?

The GRE stands for the **G**raduate **R**ecords **E**xamination. It is a standardized, national test offered by Educational Testing Services. It is an admissions requirement for most graduate programs across the United States.

DO I NEED TO TAKE IT?

Probably. If you're applying to more than one school, chances are you'll need to take the GRE. There are a few programs that don't require a GRE score. Limiting yourself to applying only to programs that do not require the GRE because you are afraid of the test is *not* an advisable strategy.

What score should I get?

I wish I had the definitive answer. Unfortunately, it depends on the program you're applying to and the other people applying the same year as you. If you earned a 300 (which is a good score) but everyone else in the applicant pool earned a 320, your "good score" is actually below average for that university's program. But in the applicant pool for a different university the average is a 295. Now your score is slightly above average. The strength of your score will vary based on the other applicants.

You gotta study hard and get the best possible score you can.

This chapter is an overview about the GRE. But the test is updated frequently and requires technical expertise that is beyond the scope of this guide. I will discuss my testing experience, how I boosted by score, and four general steps to boosting your GRE score.

Some Tips for Test Day

- Get a good night's sleep for several nights before the exam.
- Eat a healthy breakfast that will keep you full
- USE the scratch paper
- For math, use the scratch paper to work out equations and keep track of numbers
- For multiple choice questions, write out the possible answers in order (A, B, C, D, E) on your scratch paper. Physically cross off any answers that you know are wrong. This small and simple act has a big mental impact in decluttering your thought process.
- Don't be afraid to ask for more scratch paper
- Use the breaks to stretch and be physically active: Stretching keeps your blood circulating and oxygen flowing to your brain. Who cares if you look weird doing squats in your cubicle or making arm circles? You'll be thankful when

you're hitting the end of the test and you still have plenty of energy.

Five Steps to Boosting Your Score

1. Start Early:

If you're serious about boosting your score: Start Early.

I repeat, Start Early. 6 months is probably just enough time.

First of all, learn about the test. I recommend you go directly to the source: Educational Testing Service (ETS). Check out their official page on the test structure and content. Read this information carefully so you know what you're preparing for.

2. Set a date for the exam:

Think backwards from when your applications are due (December to January, probably). With that timeline, you'd want to take the GRE in November at the *latest* to allow time for the scores to be sent. If you're going to take the GRE more than once, maybe try it first in September and then again in late October or early November.

To give yourself about 6 months of practice time, you'll want to start studying around April.

Pick and register for a test date ASAP. Test dates can fill up quickly. Plus if you have a date in mind, it'll help you to stay focused on your preparation.

3. Get a Study Plan In Place A.S.A.P.

There are books, free-materials, blogs, apps, classes, and online programs all designed to prepare you for the GRE. There are even official preparation materials from ETS, the maker of the test. Each of these options has their own strengths and weaknesses, which are beyond the scope of this book.

You know yourself and your study habits. Decide your study approach quickly and get to it. Don't waste too much time switching between different plans.

Once you've figured out what material you're going to use as a base, you want to set a *realistic* study schedule. Two hours a day is probably *not* going to happen. Shoot for something more reasonable like 30-45 minutes per day and longer on the weekends. If you're consistent, the effort will pay off.

You may need to re-arrange some things in your life to make this happen, but it is worth it. Consistency in your studying is the key to improving your GRE scores. You're not trying to cram a few random factoids into your head— you're trying to expand your vocabulary and sharpen your math skills. You can't do that overnight. You *need* at least six months of regular study in order to have any meaningful impact on your scores.

4. Stick To It and Just Do it!

ONCE you've got a study program and a schedule, STICK TO IT!

It won't help you at all to pay for a program or order a book if it just sits on your shelf gathering dust. You have to USE IT!

5. Take a Practice Test

THE GRE is a LONG test. It requires physical, emotional, and mental stamina. The best way to build your stamina is by taking practice tests under real testing conditions. Taking a practice test (or two!) is an absolute must in preparing for the GRE.

If you suffer from test anxiety, completing practice tests under realistic conditions is a time-tested strategy to help. Another is to visit the testing center before test day (even more than once!) and familiarize yourself as much as possible with the building and space.

HOW I BOOSTED MY SCORE 17 POINTS

From the first time I took the GRE to the second, I raised my GRE score by 17 points with a few months of specialized, focused studying and a paid tool called Magoosh.

Magoosh is a paid, online test preparation program. They offer prep programs for many exams, including the GRE. Their programs are accessible (available 24/7 online), and they have stellar email support. I personally used it several times when I didn't understand the information and when I had technical problems. Magoosh is also very effective. They design brilliant study-materials and track your progress to adapt your studying. It helps turn your weaknesses into strengths. Best of all, Magoosh is affordable. As of the date of publication, Magoosh offers plans ranging from $149-$179; they regularly go on sale.

On my website, www.thespeechblog.com/GRE I discuss more of my experiences with the GRE and how I used Magoosh to raise my score.

Full disclosure and a favor to ask: I strongly recommend Magoosh because it helped me raise my score by 17 points. Because I recommend it so strongly, Magoosh made me an "affiliate" which means I receive a small commission for any sales I send there way. So, If you are considering using Magoosh, please visit my website (www. thespeechblog.com/magoosh) and use the link there to purchase your plan so I can receive credit for the referral.

FINAL THOUGHTS ON THE GRE

Give yourself plenty of time to prep. One week of prep isn't going to have much of an impact. You need a minimum of 2 to 3 months, but it is best to try for 6 months. If you put in the effort, you absolutely *can* raise your score.

The discipline to study every day for a set period of time is more important than fancy preparation tools or using the latest prep books.

The GRE is just *one* part of your overall application. Do not let it consume your every thought and iota of energy. Remember, it is *one* part of your application.

ABOUT THE AUTHOR

Michael Campbell is a practicing, bilingual speech-language pathologist. He earned his master's in the same area at The University of New Mexico where he also worked as a research assistant on projects related to bilingual language assessment. Additionally, Michael served as a graduate teaching assistant for *Medical Spanish* and *Introductory Spanish* courses. When Michael isn't working with clients or writing for TheSpeechBlog.com, he spends time with his husband traveling.

His experience in admissions: Michael worked for four years with Truman State University's *Upward Bound* program, coaching high school students on academic success and how to get into college. He also served as a *Career Mentor* to undergraduate students in the same university, helping them to improve their resumes and interviewing skills. As a former Fulbright Scholar, Michael served for several years on the in-country selection committee for various *Fulbright-García Robles* scholarships.

Made in the USA
Middletown, DE
01 September 2022

72911018R00066